THE WARRIOR KING

ANNA ROUNTREE

The Warrior King by Anna Rountree
Published by Charisma House, an imprint of Charisma Media
600 Rinehart Road, Lake Mary, Florida 32746

For more Spirit-led resources, visit charismahouse.com and the author's website at annarountree.com.

Cataloging-in-Publication Data is on file with the Library of Congress.

International Standard Book Number: 978-1-63641-265-8
E-book ISBN: 978-1-63641-266-5

23 24 25 26 27 — 987654321
Printed in the United States of America

Most Charisma Media products are available at special quantity discounts for bulk purchase for sales promotions, premiums, fund-raising, and educational needs. For details, call us at (407) 333-0600 or visit our website at www.charismamedia.com.

To my heavenly Father, my eternal husband, Jesus, and my ever-faithful friend, the Holy Spirit.

CONTENTS

PREFACE

WE OFTEN THINK that it is the devil that causes us the most trouble in our Christian life. Actually, we limp toward maturity in Christ due to our flesh.

The first book in this trilogy, *The Heavens Opened*, gives us the heavenly encounters we experience as we seek to know our Father. The second book in the trilogy, *The Priestly Bride*, gives to us the romance of our Savior and King with the believer. This book takes us through steps laid out before us by the Holy Spirit as He carries us into and hopefully through various tests that our heavenly Father uses to apply the cross to our flesh. Holding our flesh to the cross permits Christ to rush in and inhabit more of our soul life.

The Trinity in each of its capacities helps to empty the believer and then fill the believer by testing and training each one so that each is given the opportunity to grow up into a Christ-filled believer.

When Steve Hill, the evangelist of the great Brownsville Revival, was brought back from the dead by God, our Lord charged him with one task and that was to warn the body of Christ against false doctrine. If God Almighty feels it is of such great importance that He brings back one of His servants from the dead to warn us, it must be important. Remember, false doctrine builds up the flesh—the exact opposite of Christianity, which holds the flesh in the place of death so that more of Christ may come forth in us.

This is, after all, what our heavenly Father wants for us. He wants to see more of Jesus in us.

The first two books were painstakingly recorded in heaven and given to you just as they were given to me. The third was reconstructed, with the Lord's help, as the journals were lost when our house burned. The visions are universal in nature, however. Christians may have variations concerning the narrative, but basically all lead to the Father, the Son, and the Holy Spirit.

Right after I began having these revelations, I had a long vision in which I was Cinderella. We were living near Bob Jones (the prophet) at the time, and so I asked him about it. He brushed the revelation away with a wave of his hand. "Oh yes," he said. "I had that vision in the 1970s."

"What?" I exclaimed. "Are these visions like training wheels?"

But, you see, they are. So many people have said they have had similar revelations. We are, after all, one. All God's children are connected—not only to Him but to one another.

We all seek our heavenly Father. We all wish to draw closer to our heavenly husband, Jesus, and we all must allow the cross to hold our flesh in the place of death in order that Christ may be all in all.

Chapter 1

IRON CITY

It was the pitiless end of the first age of the world.[1] Day had abandoned its post. Night inked both land and sky. Mankind, for all its bravado, busied itself with petty feuds, mindless of the silent beast[2] that already had eaten and now was digesting it.

I Found Myself

I found myself on an embankment overlooking a bog. Huge wheels and hulls of massive equipment were half-sunk or piled in the mire mid rust-coated water and plants. It was a salvage dump for a civilization once known for its inventiveness, now known for its waste.

A massive cliff city of iron lay beyond the bog—rusted.

---

1 The world. The second age is described in Revelation 21:1: "Then I saw a new heaven and a new earth; for the first heaven and the first earth passed away, and there is no longer any sea"; see also Isaiah 65:17; 66:22: "'For behold, I create new heavens and a new earth; and the former things will not be remembered or come to mind....For just as the new heavens and the new earth which I make will endure before Me,' declares the Lord."

2 Satan

Its unoiled wheels grated loudly. A cloud of red dust suffocated its internal streets and its recessed buildings.

Years before, much of mankind had fled to iron-fortified cliffs such as these and continued life as though the corrupt evening of the world had not overtaken it. Here, crows perched atop the bog's silenced machinery calling to one another a false tattoo that all was well.

SUDDENLY

Suddenly the ground lurched violently beneath me, throwing me onto my hands and knees, knocking the breath out of me. I gasped, struggling to fill my lungs with the bitter, metallic air.

BELOW

Below, the ground of the bog split open like a ripe melon. One after another, the huge pieces of machinery tipped as though they were behemoths stumbling into the cavernous opening.

The fire within the rift looked like a smelter's furnace, with the iron of the rusted machinery adding to its eerie glow. Stagnant water joined the machinery, causing a fry of steam to rise from the molten depths.

IRON CITY

In the nearby cliff city, people crammed onto balconies or packed open windows to gape. Many screamed when they saw large, hyena-faced demons coming up from the molten depths and clambering over the falling equipment. These beasts were powerful, swift, and hungry. They headed for the city.

At the same time, dark rope ladders uncurled from the second heaven, allowing sinewy, black demons to climb down. Grappling hooks were slung over their backs so that they could pull themselves over and climb into the iron city once they reached their destination.

The cliff dwellers were trapped.

Bone-splitting shrieks rose from the besieged city. Horrific! Animal reflex snapped me into a low crouch, ready to run.

The Army

It was then that I saw a large straggle of soldiers trudging across a nearby ridge. They were led by a line of exceedingly old men clad in various pieces of armor. These were riding massive draft horses that looked like they had just been unhitched from the plow to carry these elderly fighters into battle.

The soldiers were in tatters, armed with rakes, shovels, hoes, and other nonaggressive tools. The Elders leading them seemed battle-worn and as ancient as the pieces of rusted armor they wore. Each Elder held aloft a staff from which a faded canvas insignia popped in the agitated air. I could barely make out the names of the various Christian denominations that once emblazoned the fabric.

The Far City

The sky was black with great red streaks across it as though some animal's claw had wounded it. The sounds of explosions were rolling over the ridge in waves, with a vast dust storm moving in. I squinted my eyes and held up my hand to shield them as I sought to look in the direction of the sounds.

Far in the distance, a large city was under—what looked like—nuclear attack, and the blasts of air rolling over us were from atomic explosions.

As if they were not able to see or were too stunned to understand, the Elders moved toward the bombings in the city. Flesh-melting slaughter awaited them.

No

Involuntarily I bellowed "No!" as I ran toward them, waving my arms in a warning to stop. I struggled to run fast enough to reach the last Elder in the line.

"Stop!" I cried.

"We cannot," the Elder shouted back. The Elder did not look below at the hyena-faced demons swarming toward the cliff city, but I did.

I paused a moment, looking behind, as the demons began to scale the slick outer walls. The inhabitants of the cliff city were screaming down at them and throwing anything they could lay their hands on to stop them. It was gut-wrenching but far beyond my help. I shuddered as I turned to continue my run toward the Elders on horseback.

"O God," I choked under my breath, stumbling toward the line. With a final heave, I reached the last of the massive, twenty-hands-high draft horses and grabbed part of its tack in a desperate attempt to steady myself. I could see that those demons would be coming for us next.

The Elder on the horse looked down and shouted, "We must rescue those in the great city."

"But you will not rescue anyone," I shouted. "They are gone. Rescue those behind you!"

Then seeing that I was determined to hang on and be dragged if necessary, he reached down, grabbed my arm, and pulled me up behind him onto the broad back of the horse.

"Look behind me," he called loudly. "We can defeat anything. There are thousands of us!" Then seeing that I was straining to turn enough to see adequately, he shouted, "Stand up! Behold our numbers."

I had never stood on the back of a horse, but in the panic of the moment I thought I might be able to stand after all. I needed whatever assurance the Elder was trying to give me. The horse did not flinch as I shakily stood on its rump.

The Thousands

Behind the Elder, I saw a vast number of men and women trying to move forward to confront the enemy. They were naively brave but poorly armed and poorly equipped. Already they were bent down by the blast of a storm that came from a city that no longer existed. The Elders did not understand because they were doing what they had always done. In the past, they had gone out in the name of Jesus; His banners went before them, His Elders led the way.

Not Like the Past

However, now we needed Jesus. We needed Him leading His army, Him guarding our flank, and Him serving as our rear guard.

This battle was too great. Now we must have the Captain of the Host leading His people.

The Elders needed to help those that were still following them and still alive. Demons were overpowering many of those on the periphery. These demons quickly stifled the warriors' screams by swarming over and then into them. I remembered seeing nature films of army ants swarming over prey—thousands piling on at once, viciously attacking and devouring them in seconds.

Such was about to be our fate. We were not prepared for this level of warfare, nor were the Elders.

Help

From the midst of mounting catastrophe, I looked up to heaven and cried out, "Father, help us!"

Suddenly a huge hand of light reached down from above and began lifting me out of the encroaching slaughter. Exiting the killing zone in this way, I could see further and further afield.

The whole world seemed to be burning. The cries of those being terrorized pierced my sensibilities.

"Father!" I shouted into the void.

In the blink of an eye, I went from darkness into blazing light. Unceremoniously, I was plunked down before my Father's throne.

Chapter 2

THE COMMISSION AND THE FAMILY SWORD

Brilliant with light was the throne and He who sat upon it. I seemed exceedingly small as I gazed up into the dazzling light that hid my heavenly Father's face. His chest, arms, legs, and feet glowed with an equal inner light; His flowing garment spilled out onto the sea of glass.

I dropped to my knees with my face to the floor.

"Daddy," I said in a choked whispber.

"We have been waiting for you," He said.

"Daddy." I lifted my head slightly. "Terrible things are happening on earth."

"And what are you going to do about them?"

"Me?" I gasped in shock. I looked up and saw Jesus standing to the right of our heavenly Father. Jesus was clothed in gleaming silver armor and was intent on my answer. Before Him was a huge sword on which He rested both of His hands. He seemed primed for battle and concerned about the loss of any minute given to discussion instead of action.

"Who am I, Daddy?"

"Who indeed?" He replied.

Jesus spoke: "Anna, you cannot defeat the supernatural with bullets or bombs. This enemy is immortal."

"We must do something," I pleaded.

"We are preparing a counterattack right now—but with supernatural weapons, which we issue to our family."

"And," my Father said, "I see that you yourself are not wearing your armor."[1]

"Oh," I said, looking down at myself.

He continued, "All receive armor when they come into the Kingdom—but not everyone puts it on."

I felt a bit sheepish.

---

1 According to Ephesians 6:11–19, we are commanded to put on the full armor of God as a protection against the enemy: "Put on the full armor of God, so that you will be able to stand firm against the schemes of the devil. For our struggle is not against flesh and blood, but against the rulers, against the powers, against the world forces of this darkness, against the spiritual forces of wickedness in the heavenly places. Therefore, take up the full armor of God, so that you will be able to resist in the evil day, and having done everything, to stand firm. Stand firm therefore, HAVING GIRDED YOUR LOINS WITH TRUTH, and HAVING PUT ON THE BREASTPLATE OF RIGHTEOUSNESS, and having shod YOUR FEET WITH THE PREPARATION OF THE GOSPEL OF PEACE; in addition to all, taking up the shield of faith with which you will be able to extinguish all the flaming arrows of the evil one. And take THE HELMET OF SALVATION, and the sword of the Spirit, which is the word of God. With all prayer and petition pray at all times in the Spirit, and with this in view, be on the alert with all perseverance and petition for all the saints, and pray on my behalf, that utterance may be given to me in the opening of my mouth, to make known with boldness the mystery of the gospel."

Readied for the Battle

"You wish to help? Very well. Stand to your feet," my Father said. "Fit her for battle," He called to a nearby angel.

Immediately that angel and others stepped forward carrying pieces of shining armor like Jesus'. These angels also were attired in armor. I wondered if all of heaven was preparing for war. My Father continued to speak even as He watched them buckle me into each piece.

"This armor must be tested before you go into battle alongside My Son."

"To the battle below?" I asked.

"In order to serve, you must be prepared," He stated. "When the armor is tested, you will be ready."

The Family Sword

"Hand her Our sword," my Father called. A ripple of sound ran through those on the sea of glass. Then He addressed me: "You were given a sword for writing—but for battle, you will need the sword of the Spirit."

Reverently, armored angels brought the sword and knelt before Him. He lifted the sword, which shone in His hands and amazingly sang out. It seemed as though it could not hold back the joy of being in the Father's hands. There was equal delight from those on the sea of glass. He lowered the sword and handed it to me. It was both heavy and light at the same time—heavy with His glory but light in the handling. I sheathed the sword.

He paused as if sizing up the situation. A tight smile came to Jesus' face.

THE ANGEL RUACH

My Father turned to a large, armored angel standing to His left. He must have been six feet, eight inches in height, but I could not see His face. My Father continued: "Ruach will go with you; He is both family and friend and will strengthen you in times of need."[2]

The tall angel stepped forward. The other angels showed Him deference as He took His place at attention by my right side. Though I could not see His face, His body and armor were translucent. Great power emanated from Him, and His bearing seemed more than that of an angel's. He stood at attention like a military man.

THE CALL

"Now," my Father said in a manner used to transition from one subject to another. It was as though my arrival had broken into court business, and He was ready to reengage it. "As to the matter that has been brought before Us, whom shall I send, and who will go for Us?"[3]

---

2 Ruach, the Holy Spirit, stands to the left of the Father. He may appear as an angel at times, as does Jesus. The Holy Spirit is the third person of the Trinity, equal to the Father and the Son. Therefore, He is family. He is also known as a friend because He assists us in every way. The Holy Spirit can come alongside us but will also be within us—when we make Christ our Savior and Lord. The Holy Spirit within us increases when the child of God asks to be "baptized" in the Holy Spirit.

3 Isaiah 6:8: "Whom shall I send, and who will go for Us?"

I realized that He had moved on to broader concerns, concerns of the Kingdom—perhaps of the world. What He asked sounded vaguely familiar...then I remembered the call that went out in heaven in Isaiah's day when Isaiah boldly answered before the others assembled, saying, "Here am I. Send me!"[4] And he who was not a part of the heavenly court was allowed to go. Could I do the same? Suddenly I felt emboldened and flushed with the thought that I might be able to help.

THE ANSWER

"I will go, Father," I said in the zeal of the moment.

"You, Anna?"

There was a rustle among the angels and the redeemed.

Jesus spoke to clarify the mission. "Anna, we need an emissary that will extract a beneficence that was locked away in Our garden when it was shut to mankind and its entrance guarded. After the flood it was taken and hidden in black caves. This was many years ago. In this hour we have need of it for the coming battle."

"Now that you have heard the need, Anna, do you still wish to go?" my Father asked.

"Yes!" I exclaimed, hardly able to contain my excitement. Then I thought, "Where is it?"

"Stolen," Jesus said, reading my mind. "We received a taunt this very day."

4 Isaiah 6:8

THE ENEMY'S TAUNT

A taunt?[5] Who was arrogant enough to taunt the living God to His face? I remembered that the enemy used taunts in biblical times. But this would not unnerve God Almighty. It was an affront, that's what it was—Satan was mocking our God. I felt a fury growing in me even as David did when the giant challenged the God of Israel, mocking Him.

Jesus lifted a scroll. "May I, Father?" He must have received an assurance from our Father because He read:

> Where midnight sun is swallowed by the
> vanities of men
> Cradled by a bitter root, warmed by serpent's
> skin—
> Deeper than the brave will go
> Hid where worms may seek
> The beatific, priceless prize
> Found only by the meek.
> We mock You high and lowly One.
> You ruler of the weak.
> Eternal chains await them all
> Your spineless, gutless meek.

A wave of consternation ran through those assembled.

5 A taunt is a reproach in a sarcastic, insulting, or jeering manner: to mock. It also provokes through insulting jibes. Jeremiah 24:9: "I will make them a terror and an evil for all the kingdoms of the earth, as a reproach and a proverb, a taunt and a curse in all places where I will scatter them."

"Father, it is underground," Jesus concluded.

"Anna?" my Father questioned as if giving me another chance to refuse.

"I will go," I said, now burning with indignation.

There was a cheer that went up among the redeemed. I had almost forgotten about them.

"Very well. So be it," my Father confirmed.

My Father's Cloak

My heavenly Father continued to me: "I will bestow upon you the very help you need for this challenge and beyond." Then He lifted His voice and said, "Bring forth My mantle."[6]

There was a buzz among the redeemed and also the great number of angels assembled. Angels, gold in body, hair, and clothes, brought forward a beautiful long-sleeved cloak. It shone brilliantly with bands of multi-faceted gems that caught the light with every movement. I had never seen such a glorious garment—it was truly fit for a king.

As the angels drew near, the jewels began to change. That puzzled me for the jewels became moving neon lights, rolling in a never-ending display of hot primary colors—like the marquees in Times Square, New York.

"What in the world?" I thought. "This cannot be right."

6 Mantle—a loose garment or cloak. A garment regarded as a symbol of someone's power or authority. Within the pages of this trilogy, the first mantle was received from the Holy Spirit. The second was received from Christ. The third mantle is a double-sided garment. Both the third and fourth were received from my heavenly Father.

But even before the angels reached my side, I was grateful that my Father was giving me greater understanding. He was being merciful. He gave me to understand that my body could not survive the shock of wearing His mantle immediately because I was still flesh. He had to "step it down" until I matured enough to be able to withstand the increased power.

My Father spoke: "As you complete the stages of your training, the moving lights will become jewels from My own crown. Only when you have completed the last test will the mantle properly represent Me. But you are never to use My glory to create your own."

Then, as if that was not amazing enough…

Inside Out

Suddenly, the angels turned the robe inside out—thereby displaying another garment entirely. The Father's mantle was double-sided. This side was a drab, worn, camel skin—probably as John the Baptist wore in the desert.

"Let Me help you, Anna," Jesus said. He stepped to my back and helped me put on the double mantle.

I noticed that the drab cloak completely covered the gleaming armor I now wore. The cloak left me looking like a wandering vagrant. (It is funny what you think about in times like these. I found myself grateful that the skin did not smell like a goat.)

At first I thought it strange that the ruler of the universe would wear such a drab garment. Then it came to me that our heavenly Father was as Jesus showed Him to be—humble. Of course—of course! I understood, not only the reason for wearing it, but also I understood more about my Father's character. This revelation made me even more grateful for the mantle—honored and blessed, really. If I sought that which only the meek could find, how desperately did I need to put on the humility of Christ?

The Commission

"Step forward," my Father said. I stepped closer into His blazing light. He placed His hands on my shoulders, and lightning shot through me. "Go forth," He said, "in Our authority and return to Our army that which was taken illegally by the enemy."

Great power continued to surge through me. I tingled as though electricity was running through my veins.

The Blessing

"Bless you, My child," He said. Then He removed His hands. I leaned into the light, overpowered by His love and also very light-headed. I hugged the lower part of His garment.

"Ruach," He said to the faceless angel, "take care of her." The angel bowed His head and then helped me to be more of a soldier by pulling me away. I squared my shoulders, clumsily standing at attention before I left.

Jesus smiled at me.

Ruach and I were gone.

Chapter 3

THE TREE THAT GROWS OUT OF HELL

Darkness—I could not see where Ruach had taken me. There was a dank smell—like mold from a closed, wet cellar.

The Lord's Sheepfold

"We will begin here, Anna," Ruach said in a hushed tone.

My eyes began to adjust to the deep gloom. We were in the Lord's sheepfold in mid-heaven. It was a safe "keep" provided by the Lord for His own in that corrupted stratum. A chill ran through me. I knew I could not be attacked here, but I felt exposed—like being in a glass house with an axe murderer prowling around outside.

Involuntarily, I stepped backward. As the back of my legs touched the lone bench in the area, I half stumbled, half fell onto the low seating.

After I escaped from the trophy room on my last

visit, I knew I was marked. Probably, the demons still had my scent.

Instructions

Ruach did not address my concerns but began His instructions: "You will wear the cloak of invisibility that you received above, but not the shoes."

I had received the cloak when I first went to heaven, along with a pair of shoes. Both rendered me invisible. But those shoes had no soles in them. That was to allow me to touch the heavenly realm. But now I needed protection from all parts of this corrupted stratum. I needed the shoes provided in the sheepfold. Without looking, I reached beneath the bench for the shoes I had worn before. As soon as my hand felt what seemed to be porpoise skin, I pulled them out and began to put them on my feet.

"Do not fear, Anna," Ruach continued, "they will not see us or smell us or hear us, for I will speak to you inside your spirit—where they are not granted access."

As I finished donning the shoes, I looked up nervously.

"If you are ready, we will go," He said in a gentle tone.

I smiled into His faceless face and stood. Then I took a deep breath, and as I exhaled, we were invisible.

In the Enemy's Camp

Immediately, as if we were sucked backward through a tube, Ruach set us down in what seemed to be the main hallway of some enormous structure. He had not said where we were going. But since I was turned backward, I used that advantage to get my bearings. I could see through an open doorway part of the vast moat that encircled Satan's castle. My breath caught. "O God," I said within myself, "we are right in his castle."

I felt a hand upon my shoulder and heard Ruach's calming voice: "Steady, Anna."

I took a deep breath. I wanted to believe that I could pass through this unscathed. Therefore, I settled down and focused my attention on my surroundings.

The Hall of Bones

The walls and ceilings of the hallway were intricately decorated with human bones...even chandeliers of thousands upon thousands of human bones. It was an ossuary.[1] It would have been strikingly beautiful if it had not been so ghoulish. Oil-burning containers by the hundreds lit the dark, dank hall and the rooms that we passed. There was a strange smell. It wasn't whale oil that was being burned. I believe it was oil from reconstituted human fat. The floors were an iron patchwork of stepping stones, but instead of a masonry grout linking them together, the narrow spaces were like open veins where streams of blood were running.

With so much blood openly flowing, there was a cloying smell in the air—like the sickening smell of a

1 Ossuary—a place or receptacle for the bones of the dead. The word *ossuary* comes from the late Latin *ossuarium* (from the Latin *Os*: bone).

slaughterhouse. Also, oozing from between the bones in the walls were pockets of pus and rivulets of blood. The blood and pus oozed slowly into a trough at the base of the wall and then ran along like a lumpy, slow river skirting the walls—so that the stench of death was everywhere. Ghastly.

THE ROTUNDA

Suddenly we entered what looked like an enormous rotunda with many dark passageways leading from it, twisting and turning into the shadows.

THE TREE THAT GROWS OUT OF HELL

The top of a huge tree took up a good deal of the space. It was in full leaf and had large sacs of fruit hanging from its branches. The fruit was like none I had ever seen though. It made me ill to look at it—for it was flesh, raw flesh...and the blood that was traveling throughout the castle was going into the branches that supplied this fruit.

Ruach spoke to me: "This is the blood of aborted children and those sacrificed on the altar of Satan. Even as prayers rise to God, unrighteous slaughter empowers the fallen one."

Within the expansive hall, thrones were set up with one throne elevated on a mound of human skulls. These thrones were also created from human bones, with black velvet cushions to soften their sharp edges.

THE FALLEN PRINCE

There, brooding on the elevated throne, was the evil, fallen angel himself. He had black hair that glinted with greens and blues like raven feathers, and he wore black velvet. The velvet must have been impregnated with jewels, for the gems caught the light with each movement. He had unwholesomely long, sharp nails that appeared unclean from digging into putrid flesh, it looked like, for there was a stench about them.

His clothing may have been elegant, but flies crawled freely in and out of all open areas: nose, mouth, corners of the eyes. I shivered in revulsion. It made me wonder what diseases were hidden beneath that finery. But you knew, if you were close enough, that all the finery in the world would not cover the smell of rot.

His chin was propped up with one hand, and the other hand was soundlessly drumming those overly long nails.

Strangely, his face was beautiful...cold...dangerous... devoid of light, but beautiful.

With laser-like focus, he listened to the cries coming from the blood of those sacrificed to him. He was poised like an animal ready to pounce—tense.

Then he smiled—a ghastly grimace—and as if he were a black hole, he sucked all light into himself—all joy, peace, love, hope, and expectancy.

FALSE GODS

Suddenly a cacophony of sounds shrilled through the passageways—blasting the tormented silence. I turned to look toward the conflicting sounds. In all their feathered and jeweled finery, false gods began to crowd the entry halls, their personal musicians saluting their arrival with all manner of instruments—unfortunately, loudly playing different music at the same time, therefore clashing as they tried to outdo one another. It was music played as a weapon.

There were so many high demons crowding into my sight that I could only mentally register a few.

THE COUNCIL

Pushing its way down the hall was a gargantuan three-headed monstrosity. One head was a cat's, one a frog's, and one a man's wearing a crown. Their necks went right into an engorged, saclike body on hairy spider's legs. The demon was so satiated with blood that its round cushion of a body dragged on the floor.[2]

The next was a naked man with bat's wings riding a dragon.[3] He held a snake in his right hand and wore a

---

2 This demon is considered a primary prince of the East. He is said to command sixty legions and to speak with a hoarse voice. **Note:** The names of the various high demons described in this chapter are intentionally left out, following the admonition of Scripture: "Now concerning everything which I have said to you, be on your guard; and do not mention the name of other gods, nor let them be heard from your mouth" (Exod. 23:13).

3 This demon holds the rank of duke and commands forty legions. He is a prince of the demonic order of Accusers and Inquisitors.

crown. Another demon crowded past the dragon. He had a man's body, clad in armor, with legs like coiled snakes and a head of a rooster.[4]

One had five cloven-hoofed animal legs in a circle with a furious lion's head in the center (without a torso).[5] Another demon was wearing a crown and a uniform while riding a prancing red horse.[6] One was a huge fly,[7] and on and on they came.

All—all were ghastly to behold. I realized that these false gods would inspire love in no one—only fear. Their worshippers would be paying homage to them in hopes that they would avoid reprisal. Their followers lived cowed lives…miserable…scraping together payoffs to cruel overlords, hoping against hope that they would be spared—from what?

The Conspirators

Satan raised his body on the throne and spoke so quietly that I could barely hear him: "Silence."

The sound of the clashing instruments and noisy drumming stopped.

---

4 This is a Gnostic false god. He carries a whip in one hand and a shield in the other. He is often depicted on amulets.

5 This demon is a president in hell and tenth of the seventy-two spirits identified by Solomon. He commands fifty legions and teaches logical arts that bypass God.

6 This demon was once a prince of the order of cherubim and now serves as grand pontiff in hell. He presides over twenty-six legions of demons and notarizes pacts with the devil. Like all demons, he is known to be a liar.

7 This demon was originally an idol of the Canaanites. His name means "Lord of the Flies." He causes humans to worship demons and is said to reign over witches' sabbats.

Instantly, the hideous creatures began to change before my eyes.[8] They morphed into tall, gaunt angels dressed in black, heavy with gold and bejeweled with ceremonial regalia that I supposed showed their rank in this demonic realm. As they moved toward their thrones, they reached for the low-hanging fruit from the tree. It was as casual a gesture as selecting hors d'oeuvres from a party platter. It was chilling to watch them bite into the flesh dripping with blood. I had to look away, for they consumed the flesh with such relish.

Satan observed them carefully. I could feel the tension between them all. Many of them had taken over parts of the others' territories by fomenting wars and aggressions on the earth. These fallen angels were not friends. They ruled by control, domination, and terror. Guile and bitter gall had poisoned them. They had stabbed each other in the back as often as they dared and would bring down Satan if any one of them got the chance. They only worked together because together they were more powerful. In watching them, you felt that they were working together now to bring down their great enemy, our God, but after they had taken dominion, they would fight among themselves for rule.

Satan waited until they reached their seats. When they did, all was still—the type of stillness that has condemnation hanging in it.

---

8 Actually, it was three high fallen angels.

THE COUNCIL MEETING

As if in response to Satan's mood, the flies left him and found more hospitable grazing on the bloody fruit.

There was silence.

"Why did we lose?" Satan finally asked quietly.

None answered. He lifted his head and looked at them one by one: "Their fool of a relative was tricked by his own rib. Who could be so stupid, and these are that fool's descendants?" He shook his head in disbelief. "We had them—the whole world."

One of the ashen-faced high demons showed enough courage to answer: "The Nazarene."

"Nonsense," Satan snapped, "they don't listen to Him. They spout His name and pervert His ways."

"But—" another false god began.

"But?" Satan's tone dripped with sarcasm. "Are you going to whine? Mankind is dense; all we need to do is distract them—then disqualify them." He threw up his hands and shrugged. "You were lax."

"Kill them," came a guttural growl from a throne further away from Satan's.

"Yes." Satan smiled and gave a low chuckle. Then, as if talking to himself, he muttered distractedly, "But we do not need to kill them to neutralize them." He dropped his head backward for a few seconds, smiling and savoring the idea of actually killing mankind—instead of using the longer way of manipulating them. "I would like to kill them, but…" he said. A chuckle ran through the room. Everyone knew how he felt and savored the idea with him.

"We almost had a worldwide cartel," another added wistfully.

Satan rolled his eyes over in the direction of that high demon, and with exaggerated pronunciation, popping his consonants, said, "But we didn't."

"Do we need something new?" a demon asked, naively.

"No," Satan scoffed. "They do not live long enough to learn anything from life. They are so dense; they would need to see our tactics over many lifetimes to learn anything. We will undermine them from within, as we have always done."

Groans came from the demons. Overriding the groans, like a parent with recalcitrant teens, he continued: "We will pack our forces into the spaces given over to us—then, eat them from within. As we corrupt them, we will block out the light. They will be shouting at us from without, but we will be conquering them from within." He chuckled, "Their enemy is already in the camp."

There was a glum resistance to this pep talk that was the same as it had always been. Always!

"Do we get no rewards for weakening these dolts?" asked a demon that looked like a peacock when he arrived.[9] This was such a mild retort that it was surprising that such a statement would gather those present into a unified expression of disapproval.

9 A chieftain in hell, possibly the Sumerian sun god, which was worshipped by burning children as a sacrificial offering.

A droning sound began, like the unity of bees in a hive.

From the quickness of the unified response, you could tell they had been meeting behind their leader's back.

This unity emboldened another: "Drugs are like party favors now. We are poisoning them—dulling them down."

Then another blurted, "We have made perversions acceptable, desirable even."

The hum continued and increased. It was as if they were growing in strength by exposing their hidden numbers.

"Millions are aborted. Their parts carved up and sold," another squalled.

They seemed to be on a roll. More of their numbers were willing to expose their common bond without Satan.

"We have corrupted their governments until the leaders celebrate their own crimes," a high demon said giddily with his new freedom of risking reprisal. For no reason, he began to laugh. "And the people are demoralized. They feel helpless to make changes."

They all started laughing in some sort of frantic release.

And Religion

"And religion!" A whoop went up from those assembled. "Most of them are worshipping us under the guise of deeper revelations found in hidden sources," another scoffed.

Their cheer in response was a little over the top.

"Yes," Satan agreed, raising his voice above theirs. "We almost had them."

"Worldwide," a demon shouted, playing to the crowd. Everyone clapped.

"Yes, worldwide—then..." Satan buckled down into a low growl.

The levity stopped.

"And then we didn't." His words dripped with acid.

Quietly at first, the drone began again—this time in deliberate protest. Then one of the high demons whispered defiantly, "The Nazarene"—rebelling against Satan's displeasure.

"Don't say His name!" Satan blurted far too loudly. All of this was getting to him. Mainly it was the realization that they had been meeting behind his back.

Then like a naughty child, from the back of the room, another voice slipped in the name like a knife: "The Nazarene."

"Don't say His name!" Satan screamed.

Quickly, like a pack of wild dogs circling their prey, several more goaded Satan under their breaths, saying, "The Nazarene, the Nazarene."

Amid this growing, gut-churning verbal attack and its implications, I heard a young child crying, "Help me!"

I looked around. Ruach touched my arm, indicating it was time to go.

"Help me!" came the cry again. Quickly, I realized that the cry did not come from this room.

"Come, Anna," Ruach said with urgency in His voice. He was right; the mood was becoming dangerous.

Strident alarm and anger was becoming violent rage. Their collected fury was affecting the room itself.

Blood started oozing from the walls and dripping from the leaves of the tree and its fruit. Then terrifying, heavy darkness rolled in. I could hear sardonic laughter, screams of pain, and the drone changed into an open chant defying Satan: "The Nazarene, the Nazarene."

Smaller demons began to leap from the safety of the inner walls and frantically rushed about trying to get out—like rats jumping ship.

Ruach grabbed my hand. The floor disappeared from beneath us, and swiftly we began to slide downward through the trunk of the tree.

Chapter 4

THE GIRDLE OF TRUTH

My breath was coming in fits and starts as we spiraled down the inner wood of that massive tree. I tried to catch my breath. I consoled myself with the exhilarating fact that we had escaped. Granted, we dropped out of there like being dispatched through a trap door—but we were safe.

The Descent

Even as I accustomed myself to a controlled slide downward, I looked at my surroundings. I had no idea where we were going, but Ruach did not seem worried, so I supposed that this was part of the plan.

Intermittently, smaller demons passed us, flying upward. They were intent on reaching their destination, and we were still invisible.

As we slid further from those fallen angels, I began to ruminate on what I had seen in the castle. I believe I was too stunned at first to understand the implications of what I was seeing. I always thought Satan had a vise-like grip on all the participants of his organization. But now I saw that, in reality, it was difficult to control them. Rebellion breeds rebellion. If he turned on God, others would turn on him.

Not only was I stunned by their undercutting of a leader whom they feared, but I also realized Satan was losing control over those under him. He had become scattered, stale. I saw clearly that he had been away from the Light—He who is Life and the source of all fresh, clear thinking. Therefore, he could only repeat his former plans and actions over and over again. He was right; mankind was simple. But we were not going to be fighting this battle—Jesus was. Only He could win against such an old, wily foe as Satan.

THE INSIDE OF THE TREE

I began to look at the contents of that hollow tree as I passed downward. Jewels encrusted the inner trunk—but I could tell that they were not real. They did not have the luster. Other desirable "gets" were handily available: furs (fake), gold (fake…it had to be), even antiques and oil paintings (all fake, I was sure). There were stacks of fake Dresden china and plastic for crystal, rolls of knockoff Persian rugs and plaster copies of statuary. The inside of the tree was like a warehouse of all that looked good but was worthless.[1]

What was this tree anyway? Was it the other tree in the garden? Even as the tree of life was still in the garden

---

1 The tree of the knowledge of good and evil represents the flesh nature of mankind. No matter how good it looks, it is worthless to God.

of God above, was this—? I dared to think: Was this the tree of the knowledge of good and evil?

"Of course, of course," I said to myself. "If the tree of life is above, the other tree in the garden would have its taproot plunging into hell." I had wondered where it had gone, but I knew that all that seems "good" without God is flesh.

Isaiah's Prophecy

Did I witness the first chink in the armor that eventually would lead to the disintegration of all Satan's plans of ascending to heaven and raising his throne above "the stars of God"? Had he read Isaiah's prophecy? "What am I thinking?" I asked myself. "Probably, he was listening when it was given." I thought I might be able to remember it, so I mumbled it to myself as I continued downward:

> "How you have fallen from heaven,
> O star of the morning, son of the dawn!
> You have been cut down to the earth,
> You who have weakened the nations!
> "But you said in your heart,
> 'I will ascend to heaven;
> I will raise my throne above the stars
> of God,
> And I will sit on the mount of assembly
> In the recesses of the north.
> 'I will ascend above the heights of the

clouds;
I will make myself like the Most High.'
"Nevertheless you will be thrust down to
Sheol,
To the recesses of the pit.
"Those who see you will gaze at you,
They will ponder over you, saying,
'Is this the man who made the earth
tremble,
Who shook kingdoms,
Who made the world like a wilderness
And overthrew its cities,
Who did not allow his prisoners to go
home?'"[2]

"Oh dear God," I said within myself, "what are You showing me?"

Then reality set in with sobering clarity. The unity of hate was actually fragile. All manner of treachery grows in the dark, and even as open battle was destroying the earth, in darkness Satan's kingdom was unraveling—moving all of us closer to fulfilling Isaiah's prophecy.

With a thud, we arrived at the base of the slide. Thank heavens, it was not hell as I had feared.

---

2 Isaiah 14:12–17. Even though this Scripture passage deals with a human enemy, the hidden meaning is generally believed to be a prophecy about Satan.

THE ENTRYWAY

The entryway at the bottom of the slide was a tangle of tree roots. It looked something like the rotunda from which we had escaped—but now, instead of the top of the tree, it seemed to be the root system. I wondered what fed a tree whose fruit was "the flesh." Some of the roots were so large they seemed to house rooms and multiple tunnels.

Ruach spoke out loud to me: "Do you have your footing?" He became visible (except His face). He was wearing a wheat-colored robe that hid His gleaming armor.

I answered that I did. The floor on which we were now standing was dirt.[3] Bugs and other insects were crawling in and out of the soil: worms, nightcrawlers, black beetles, spiders, and the like—those you might find if you turned over a rotted tree in the forest. The smell was moist, rich, and woodsy.

"Where are we?" I asked as I regained my equilibrium. The cloak of invisibility disappeared. "Oh goodness," I thought, "I don't want to lose that."

THE TEST

"You will not," Ruach said, reading my thoughts. He continued, "Before you join your Beloved on the field of battle, the Lord must test your armor. This is your proving ground. Until your armor is tested, you are a liability to yourself and others."[4]

---

3 We are made of dust.

4 1 Samuel 17:36–39 (NASB): "'Your servant has killed both the lion and the bear; and this uncircumcised Philistine will be like one of them, since he has

"Goodness," I said, "I don't want that. How do I test the armor?"

"You do not," He said. "The Holy Spirit applies the tests—given when you least expect them. It is up to the soldier of the cross to pass through these tests. Depending upon your heartfelt decisions, you will either move forward or be given an opportunity to try again."

"The same test?"

"The same."

"No pressure," I singsonged under my breath.

"Shall we?" asked Ruach formally with a bow. He gestured toward the massive, nearby root. The sign over the broad doorway read: "Thieves' Market."

The Thieves' Market

I quietly said, "Lord, help me," as I passed in front of Ruach to enter the poorly lit tunnel. One string of colored Christmas tree lights hung willy-nilly to provide partial illumination.

However, there was brilliant light at the end of the tunnel. Therefore, both Ruach and I increased our pace. I wanted to get to that light and the source of the joyous music and laughter up ahead.

---

defied the armies of the living God.' And David said, 'The Lord who saved me from the paw of the lion and the paw of the bear, He will save me from the hand of this Philistine.' So Saul said to David, 'Go, and may the Lord be with you.' Then Saul clothed David with his military attire and put a bronze helmet on his head, and outfitted him with armor. And David strapped on his sword over his military attire and struggled at walking, for he had not trained with the armor. So David said to Saul, 'I cannot go with these, because I have not trained with them.' And David took them off."

Quickly, we burst into a vast, bustling dome. People from all nations were everywhere: buying, trading, bartering, dancing, being whipped around in carnival rides, and eating cotton candy. The booths in the center of the floor were festive with flags, colored balloons, and blinking holiday lights. Barkers were hawking their wares at every tent and selling tickets to rides and to the attractions within the tents.

The Merchandise

Ruach and I mingled among the visitors that were gazing at and purchasing the wares. The merchandise was odd, and truly, I did not know what most of it meant or who would buy it. For sale were Soul Catchers (whatever they were), Facade Enhancers (I thought I might be able to guess at those), Veneers, Name-Dropping Classes, Vanity Tours, and Embellished Resumes. You could visit a "delusionist" the same way some people might see a fortune teller. Some of the barkers were puppeteers teaching false doctrines that tied people up and kept them dangling like marionettes.

Booths and Rides

There were kissing booths for those who wanted to court various doctrines as though they were potential marriage partners, then throw them off as soon as a new doctrine came along. There was a maze called Maze of Errors (that did not sound promising) and a stuffed pillow booth called Hug-a-Bug, where people could test the truth by squeezing the pillow to see how the truth felt to them instead of relying on the written Word. Boats were available for lazy river rides so that people could be carried downstream by their favorite opinions, and there was the House of Many Winds where people could be tossed to and fro by "every wind of doctrine." I was particularly perplexed by the Human Pretzel machines, which twisted and contorted people so that they could live for the approval of others. Deception was everywhere.

HOODED ONES

Milling in and out of those dazzled by the festivities were others who looked like hooded monks.

"Who are these?" I asked Ruach.

He answered, "Hypocrisy always wears religious robes.[5] These perform spiritual duties before others, but actually they defraud God's people."

As I watched, these false monks were apprehending one after another of those participating in the market.

---

5 Matthew 23:1–7, a passage in which Jesus exposes religious hypocrisy: "Then Jesus spoke to the crowds and to His disciples, saying: 'The scribes and the Pharisees have seated themselves in the chair of Moses. Therefore, whatever they tell you, do and comply with it all, but do not do as they do; for they say things and do not do them. And they tie up heavy burdens and lay them on people's shoulders, but they themselves are unwilling to move them with so much as their finger. And they do all their deeds to be noticed by other people; for they broaden their phylacteries and lengthen the tassels of their garments. And they love the place of honor at banquets, and the seats of honor in the synagogues, and personal greetings in the marketplaces, and being called Rabbi by the people" (NASB, see also Matthew 23:13–31 regarding the "Eight Woes.")

The monks were guiding them to dark caves on various sides of the periphery.

I pushed through the dancers on the ballroom floor doing the delirious "Dance of Death," whereby they kept themselves distracted by any means possible.

The Caves

At the edge of this frantic dance, the light grew dim and hazy. I stood very still, waiting for my eyes to adjust. Finally, I could see where the monks were leading the attendees. They were taking them into the dimly lit caves.

Within the caves, the monks had stacked cages, one on top of another. Inside these cages were hollow-eyed humans, peering out, hugging their Hug-a-Bug pillows, or repeatedly playing the Canned Applause they had bought to encourage themselves falsely.

Those in Cages

I felt pity for those who were being tricked. All the lively music, the thrill rides, the aids to besting the system were lies. Lucifer, the father of lies, was distracting and diverting the Christians and deluding the unsaved.

I turned to Ruach. "They are being duped."

"Yes," He said. "If they had taken seriously the names of the rides and merchandise, they might have shown more care. But they lied to themselves."

"Lied to themselves?"

"Yes. Only if one joins in with the enemy's lie against

himself can he be captured. He himself must overpower the voice of the Holy Spirit urging him to resist."

"But why would they not resist?" I asked.

"Ulterior motives."

My breath caught. I had made mistakes in this way. I had chosen incorrectly and been dragged off and caged so that I was stunted, unable to fulfill God's plans for my life. I had been sidetracked for years at a time.

I felt acute pain in my stomach. I bent over and cried out. There was so much noise even at the edge of the market that the cry passed for a laugh.

SOLDIER OF THE CROSS

Ruach addressed me: "Yes, your flesh hindered you in the past, but now you have no time to live according to the flesh, squandering your time here on earth. You are a soldier of the cross, and you have accepted a sacred mission from your Father. You have a job to do—we all do. The time is short. Do you feel pity for those captured and caged? Then let the Warrior King be victorious in your life, and He will rescue others through you," He concluded.

I thought, "This is a side of Ruach I have not seen. Here are the brass and steel I had expected from the army of God." But I too was a part of that army. I was being trained to fight alongside angels. Was I taking hold of the training being offered to me? Was I showing brass and steel?

I straightened my back. "Yes, I want to help, and if this armor needs to be tested first, I want it tested."

Suddenly a neon arrow appeared in front of me, squeezing in and then popping out to point to the Testing Ground.

I chuckled. "Well, that was quick."

"The way lies before you, Anna," Ruach said. Instantaneously a door appeared. A sign over the door read: "Answer and You Exit."

"That's very odd," I said out loud. "In fact, this whole market is getting stranger and stranger." I turned to smile at Ruach but found I was speaking to no one.

I paused a moment to take in the implications of that, then crossed to the door and opened it with a determined grip.

Behind the Door

It was very dark in the room to which the door gave me access. As my eyes adjusted from the market lights to the strange gloom, I realized that there were demons in black robes packed into this large area. On the walls, which I felt were moving (before I saw that they actually *were* moving), were venomous peacock spiders ready to strike.[6] Thousands of them were preening and dancing and eating one another. I pulled away from the walls.

"Come in," a computer-generated voice said. The demons parted to allow me to move forward. I cringed as

6 Peacock spiders: this species of jumping spider is found almost exclusively in Australia. They are carnivores, preferring crickets, but will eat each other. The male spider performs a colorful mating dance to attract a female. Their name comes from the rear fans that are raised and vibrated before the female during the mating dance.

I walked toward the voice, not wanting to touch anything. As I walked, I thought, "How right that in a market filled with deception and unbelief that the one addressing me would not be real."

Finally, I reached a small wooden table on which sat one of those large black eight-ball "oracles." People used them as party games years ago. Supposedly you could ask the eight-ball anything, tilt it, and it would answer.

THE ORACLE

The Oracle spoke: "You're disappointed."

"No," I protested, "I was expecting...well, I don't know what I was expecting."

"Well," the ball said archly, "I'm not just a pretty face."

"No." I half laughed at his critique of himself. This elicited hisses from the demons and threatening waves of colorful peacock behinds by the spiders.

"Oh, dear," I said. Their reaction sobered me. I think until this point I had not felt that I was in danger, but I began to feel uneasy in the pit of my stomach.

"Well," the ball snapped, "I suppose we can expect nothing better from someone like you."

I was being baited. I thought it best to let it pass.

Finally I asked, "May we proceed?"

"Don't be pushy," the Oracle seethed.

I gave a tight smile and held my ground.

THE QUESTION

The computer-generated voice cleared its throat and continued: "In your studies, you have found that throughout history most people groups develop a main god and a son of god—many even have a worldwide flood in their stories. They have different names, but all lead to generally the same conclusions. Therefore, if one is honest, Christianity is not unique. In the end all of these 'ways' are essentially the same.[7] To know this is to enter into that God-consciousness written of in Psalm 82 in the texts you follow. It says: 'You are gods.'[8] What say you?"

Internally I called out to God: "Let the Spirit of the Lord be upon me." But the Oracle was right. I had studied all the major religions. However, Christianity is not just a story meant to explain the mysteries of life; it is a relationship—a relationship with a living Person who walked the earth and is still alive in the spiritual realm. I know this Person. I know Him well, and I love Him. "Lord," I prayed within myself, "be with me now."

---

7 This is an ancient Gnostic false doctrine. The Gnostics held that revealed truth was witnessed in many religions, and the people who knew "the truth" would know the same truth. This means that salvation is by knowledge, not by the finished work of Christ on the cross. Therefore, the Gnostics believed we were already saved and just needed to get our thinking straight.

8 Psalm 82:5–8 (NASB): "They do not know nor do they understand; they walk around in darkness; all the foundations of the earth are shaken. I said, 'You are gods, and all of you are sons of the Most High. Nevertheless you will die like men, and fall like one of the princes.' Arise, God, judge the earth! For You possess all the nations."

THE ANSWER

I looked back at the Oracle. I felt the strength of the Lord's courage rising up within me. "You greatly err in your understanding of the scripture. The truth is that it is also written that Jesus clarified the meaning of this passage in John 10:35.[9] Jesus spoke of the psalmist, the writer of Psalm 82, when He said, 'He called them gods, to whom the word of God came…' In other words, that is what the psalmist was calling the prophets. There is but one God." Just saying this truth emboldened me.

I continued: "But of Himself, Jesus said: 'I am the way, and the truth, and the life.'[9] Our Father sent Him into the world to live, die, and live again to testify to the truth that He alone is the Way.[10]"

"The legends of false gods are mankind's way of explaining the story of our Savior written by our heavenly Father in the stars. But the early fathers like Adam and Noah, who knew what was being told through the stars and planets, died out, and the clear story of the Messiah written above was lost in time until Jesus Himself came to earth. He lived that which is written above. There is no other way. Just as there is no other way than the Father giving grace to someone born spiritually dead in order that they may have the

---

9 John 14:6 (NASB): "Jesus said to him, 'I am the way, and the truth, and the life; no one comes to the Father except through Me.'"

10 Jesus was "very God" and "very man." This means He is both. In the fullest sense He is God, and in the fullest sense He is man. This allowed Him to step down God's power so that it could be received by humankind. God's full power would destroy man. But when Jesus came to earth, He was a "transformer"—making the power receivable by humankind.

opportunity to choose Christ and live.[11] Today I am spiritually alive. I live because I have exchanged my 'death' for His life. There is but one way to join the family of God, and that is through Jesus, the door."

Suddenly, the girdle of truth tightened around my thighs—strengthening me to stand.

At the same time, bedlam broke out in the packed room. The hoods flew off the demons as frills flared from their necks like prehistoric lizards, and the aggressive peacock spiders attacked like lions—leaping in my direction.

THE EXIT

But I disappeared through a trap door that must have been the exit, for I shot right out into the hall where Ruach was waiting.

Still trembling as I stood, I said, "'Answer and you exit!' Thank You, Lord."

11 Grace is a spontaneous, unmerited gift of divine favor. Grace must be extended to humans to even contemplate salvation.

Chapter 5

THE BREASTPLATE OF RIGHTEOUSNESS: PART 1

The hallway laced with tree roots seemed much brighter after the interrogation room. The escape had left me shaken, but I was comforted by Ruach waiting for me. He dusted me off as if removing all that might be clinging to me after passing through the Thieves' Market.

Help on the Journey

"You did well, Anna," He said, then quickly changed gears. "Now, there is no time to waste."

"But Ruach," I cut in, "what about all those in cages?"

"Your full armor has not been tested, Anna. There may be weaknesses."

"But David went up against the giant with nothing but a slingshot."[1]

"David was not in untested armor," He said. "Besides, he had killed both the lion and the bear. Have you killed the lion and the bear?"[2]

"No," I said slowly.

"Zeal," He said, "will not take the place of zeal tempered by wisdom and training. Your time will come."

I was a bit distracted because I wanted to peek at my Father's cloak to see if there was a change. This action was interrupted, however.

TWO HELPERS

Suddenly a beautiful angel appeared before me. She looked young and fresh, with straight golden hair that flowed down her back to her heels. Her electric-white garment looked Roman—but the Rome of an earlier time,

---

1 1 Samuel 17:40 (NASB): "Then [David] took his staff in his hand and chose for himself five smooth stones from the brook, and put them in the shepherd's bag which he had, that is, in his shepherd's pouch, and his sling was in his hand; and he approached the Philistine."

2 1 Samuel 17:34–38: "But David said to Saul, 'Your servant was tending his father's sheep. When a lion or a bear came and took a sheep from the flock, I went out after it and attacked it, and rescued the sheep from its mouth; and when it rose up against me, I grabbed it by its mane and struck it and killed it. Your servant has killed both the lion and the bear; and this uncircumcised Philistine will be like one of them, since he has defied the armies of the living God.' And David said, 'The LORD who saved me from the paw of the lion and the paw of the bear, He will save me from the hand of this Philistine.' So Saul said to David, 'Go, and may the LORD be with you.' Then Saul clothed David with his military attire and put a bronze helmet on his head, and outfitted him with armor."

perhaps of the Caesars. Her sandals were as golden as her hair. Light radiated from her head, hands, and feet.

Appearing with her was a spirit about six and a half feet tall. His outline was blue, and his attire looked straight and simple. He was almost only an impression. (I say this because I could see right through him.)

Ruach continued, "I have asked these two helpers to accompany you through the areas ahead. This is Chastity and the Spirit of Counsel. You will need both to pass through the next chambers."

Both bowed their heads in recognition of being introduced. The Spirit of Counsel, seeming to have seniority, spoke: "We are honored to be given this task."

I looked quizzically toward Ruach, who responded, "The testing of the breastplate is crucial, for you must pass through the heart."

"But a heart that is resistant," added the Spirit of Counsel.

Chastity reached to check my breastplate's straps to be sure they were secure. "May I?" she inquired. I nodded my acceptance as she began to pull and yank. She added, "A heart that is hardened, divided, at times—wicked."

"You have no time to waste," interjected Ruach.

"Well then, shall we go, Anna?" the Spirit of Counsel asked.

Chastity leaned over with her hand still on one buckle of the breastplate. "Believe nothing the flesh suggests to you," she whispered.

"With the Lord's help," I answered them both, then exhaled deeply—as if readying myself for an Olympic sprint.

THE FIRST CHAMBER—THE LUST OF THE FLESH

We stepped toward the entrance of the chamber housing the next trial.

"The Lord is adding grace to you before this challenge. You now have grace upon grace," Chastity quietly confided.[3]

Before I had the time to contemplate the meaning of this, we were at the entry door. Over the doorway was a large, florid sign. It was beautifully executed with swirls of gold and scarlet. Right in the center of all this excessive swirling (and almost hidden by it) was the word "Lust."

Before I could truly register what I had seen, we were sucked forcibly into an anteroom, which I somehow knew represented the upper chamber of one side of the heart.[4] The light available came from Chastity's head, hands, and feet. Therefore, the reach of the light was shallow at best, leaving most of the chamber in a spotty half-light.

Chastity led the way so that we could walk without groping. However, as my eyes adjusted, I could see people encased in the walls. Their arms were unhindered, and their faces were partially exposed. Their eyes followed us as we passed, and they reached out in some desperate need to touch us.

3 Through unmerited kindness (grace), we are given the opportunity to come to Christ and be saved. John 1:16 says that from the fullness of the Father we have received grace upon grace. In this instance we are given Christ, but other times in our lives the Lord adds grace to us: "grace upon grace."

4 The anteroom is the upper chamber of one side of the heart.

THE LURE

Seductive whispers began to run along the wall.

"You can try it," one whispered.

"Come on, no one will know."

At first I did not understand their meaning.

"It's dark here," another chuckled seductively.

"Come on," someone urged greasily.

"No one will see you," another hissed.

I began to understand. My conscience rose to resist.

"No one," someone breathed.

"You want to know how it feels," another slimed.

The seductive tone of their voices lulled and caressed. Despite myself, it was beginning to draw me. Somehow I felt myself drift into a half stupor. Without knowing it, I moved closer to the wall. A hand brushed my arm. It felt natural, acceptable.

"Do not let them pull you, Anna," Chastity whispered.

"Come on," another urged.

"Let's," was breathed.

"You want to..." a voice chuckled.

The whispers did not bounce off me. Instead, like long, invisible fingers, they slid right into my heart.

More hands were being placed on me, soothing me—coaxing me—making me less sensitive to being defiled. They could tell I was curious.

"But it feels good..."

"Anna," the Spirit of Counsel interjected.

His voice was sidetracked, for my mind had begun to

drift. It was entertaining the idea that I could go a little further just to see how it felt, and then, before I could not stop myself, pull back.

"More," I thought.

"Anna," Chastity said out loud.

"Not all the way," I said within.

More arms were pulling me to the wall. My legs began to buckle, and my eyes glazed over.

"Anna!" A sharp tone from the Spirit of Counsel jarred.

I blinked back into reality. "I..." I scrambled internally to pull myself from the quicksand of their arms.

"Fight them," Chastity urged.

"Fight!" the Spirit of Counsel added forcefully.

I began to extract myself from the hands pulling at me, and even though my sword felt heavier than a truck, I unsheathed it. I felt weak and was struggling to catch my breath, for I was conflicted. With all the strength I could muster, I lifted the sword over my head. The room flooded with light like the noonday. Those in the walls recoiled into shadows like sea urchins retracting their tentacles from harm.

THE FIGHT

The sight strengthened me. "Stand back," I shouted huskily, "in the name of Jesus!" Then my voice became clearer and stronger as I continued: "This body is a temple of the Holy Spirit, and you will not defile it! Leave me—in Jesus' name." Holding the sword aloft, I stumbled backward, smashing into what seemed to be a valve.

Exiting

Suddenly, all three of us were sucked through this valve-like curtain that closed very firmly behind us.[5] I turned quickly to see that there was no way out. A sign on the membrane read: "No Exit."

I needed air. I bent over like a runner that had completed a hard race. I was dazed and disoriented. I understood why I needed greater grace.

The Spirit of Counsel comforted me by saying, "The next challenge will not be as difficult."

I lifted my head to look at him. "Why?" I panted.

"Because you passed the first part of the test."

As I looked up, I continued to sheath my sword. "I mean, why was that so difficult?"

"Because it was attacking your body—the house you live in," he answered, "part of your human nature, which is animal."

My spirit was bruised from the encounter. My companions could see that I needed time to catch my breath.

---

5 A valve between the upper and lower chambers of the heart. Blood enters the heart by the right atrium (represented in this book by the lust of the flesh) and passes through a tricuspid valve into the right ventricle (the chambers housing the lust of the eyes and the pride of life). From the right ventricle the passage of blood uses the pulmonary artery to the lungs (the wind tree in the book). From the lungs, the blood passes through the left pulmonary valve into the left atrium—then through the mitral valve into the left ventricle and on to the aortic valve to the aorta and then to the body.

Chastity continued, "Many believe their body is their own and they can do with it as they please."[6]

"But they are wrong," the Spirit of Counsel added. "The body is not mankind's amusement park."

"It belongs to the Lord," Chastity said. "He bought it with His blood."

His Standards

"He owns these bodies now, and therefore they are encoded with His standards.[7] Since entering the family of the living God, lasciviousness and filthiness are not a part of your spiritual DNA," the Spirit of Counsel said. "If a child of God goes against the encoded standards, self-loathing is often the result, unless your conscience is seared."

"And uncleanness disqualifies the Lord's soldier from battle—and our God needs you for the battle," Chastity added. "For this reason, He has given you His righteousness as a breastplate to cover your heart and conscience."

"For the Word says that the righteous are bold as a lion," the Spirit of Counsel said. "The enemy does not need to kill you if he can disqualify you—leave you feeling guilty, for

---

6 Romans 12:1: "Therefore I urge you, brethren, by the mercies of God, to present your bodies a living and holy sacrifice, acceptable to God, which is your spiritual service of worship"; see also 1 Corinthians 6:19–20 and Romans 1:18–32.

7 1 Corinthians 6:19–20: "Or do you not know that your body is a temple of the Holy Spirit who is in you, whom you have from God, and that you are not your own? For you have been bought with a price: therefore glorify God in your body."

the guilty are always hiding and afraid.[8] If he can disqualify you, you are as good as dead before the fight. That is the reason Satan will allow you to be anything but truly holy. The Lord needs holy warriors for a holy war."

THANKING MY COMPANIONS

"Thank you both for helping me," I said. I shook my head, trying to think of something else to say. "That was difficult."

They both put an arm around my back and sort of jostled me. "Now, Anna," they both soothed, "we are doing this together, are we not?"

"Yes," I said—then with a bit more steel up my spine, I nodded my head decisively and repeated: "Yes, we are!"

"That's the spirit!" they chimed in together.

After squaring my shoulders, I turned on my heel and faced the meadow that lay before me. The outdoor billboard read: "Welcome Goat Ropers." In smaller lettering, I saw the word "Academy" under the gargantuan welcome.

"Let's go," I said abruptly, trying to put all of "that" behind me. With decisiveness, I stepped forward. Together we began walking down into a lush meadow.

"Goat ropers, isn't that a sort of slang term for a cowboy?" I asked as we walked.[9]

---

8 1 John 2:6 (NASB): "The one who says that he remains in Him ought, himself also, to walk just as He walked."

9 A goat roper is a wannabe rancher or one posing as a cowboy.

Judas Goats

"Not these," the Spirit of Counsel said. "This is an academy to train Judas goats to rope in the sheep."

I stopped dead in my tracks. "What?" I exclaimed.

"Oh, yes," Chastity said. "The enemy finds them useful."

"But no child of God would be willing to learn how to lead their friends to slaughter," I said and then began walking again.

"Most pretend not to know. The goats don't want to know," Chastity said.

"But there is a gnawing feeling in the back of their minds," added the Spirit of Counsel.

"Still..." I shook my head. "How can anyone justify leading God's people to slaughter?"

Compromise

"Compromise," Chastity and the Spirit of Counsel said together.[10]

"They decide that getting along with mankind is more important than righteousness toward God," the Spirit of Counsel said.

"They don't want to ruffle feathers. They want everything to be 'nice,'" added Chastity. "They have convinced

10 Compromise is limping between two opinions. This is spoken of in 1 Kings 18:21: "If the Lord is God, follow Him; but if Baal, follow him." There is but one true God, one infinitely immense and incomprehensible being. God allows us to choose to follow Him or the false gods of this world. He does not want His children to compromise.

themselves that if everything is pleasant, they have fulfilled Christian love."

"And because the sheep know them and even love them…" the Spirit of Counsel said.

"Yes!" said Chastity. "Forgive me for breaking in, but Judas goats are always so loving, agreeable—attractive even—that the enemy uses them as bait to draw in others."

"To their spiritual death at times," the Spirit of Counsel added.

SHEEP LED BY GOATS

As we walked down the lush embankment, we caught sight of different pastures as the sheep moved to gather around that pasture's goat. We could tell that they loved their goat.[11]

In the distance, a goat was leading a flock of sheep. The sign on the building to which they were being led read: "Slaughterhouse."

"We must stop them!" I said with great alarm.

"No, Anna," they would not hear you," Chastity said.

---

11 Goats have been used to comfort other animals for many years. Have you ever heard the phrase "Don't let anyone get your goat"? It came from those who race horses. High-strung racehorses might stay awake all night before a race. In fact, the opposition would try to wear them down by causing them to lose sleep. But they found that a goat in the stall with the horse would comfort it and the horse would rest. Therefore, the phrase "Don't let anyone get your goat" became a standard saying. Goats also have been used to comfort sheep. But the phrase "Judas goat" came into use when the goats began to lead the unsuspecting sheep to their death.

"They can only hear their goat, for the goat's very presence makes everything seem alright."

"But—" I interjected.

"Later, Anna," the Spirit of Counsel said.

We watched as the goat led the sheep into the Slaughterhouse. Almost immediately, the goat came out of an exit on the other end. The goat was welcomed by a demon posing as a man. It was praised and given delectable treats as it too was then led away.

I said, "The goat lives another day to lead new friends to their doom."

"Yes," said Chastity.

After a pause, the Spirit of Counsel sighed, "Come, Anna." We turned to face the entrance to a garden. The walkway was flanked by two stone obelisks covered with mirrors. Beyond these lay what seemed to be an English country garden. The sign over the entrance read: "The Garden of Worldly Delights."[12]

I did not try to peek at the cloak given to me by my Father, for I was saddened by my struggle in the heart's upper chamber and concerned that the struggle had hindered in some way the conversion of the light into jewels on the Father's mantle.

"Come along, Anna," the Spirit of Counsel urged. "More awaits you in the lower chamber of the heart."

---

12 Worldly delights are the lust of the flesh, the lust of the eyes, and the pride of life.

Chapter 6

THE BREASTPLATE OF RIGHTEOUSNESS: PART 2

We entered the hedged-in Garden of Worldly Delights. It was lush, with a riot of flowers—all heights and types. Also, it was an absolute panic of colors. The Spirit of Counsel and Chastity and I stood amazed at the beauty and heavy fragrances of this country garden. With our eyes closed, we breathed in its intoxicating aromas.

Opening Our Eyes—the Lust of the Eyes

When we opened our eyes, we continued to feast—but now, with our eyes. How so many varieties and colors could blend to display God's beauty was an unexpected delight. I did not just experience the joy of the garden at that moment—it made me want to live in such beauty. It created a hunger. I shook my head to clear it from being seduced by the beauty before me.

Flowers Talking

It was then that I realized that the flowers had faces. They were talking to one another. Indeed, flower petals did encircle their faces; however, the rest of them—that is to say, their bodies—looked human. They were standing in a flowerbed together, as if they were growing in that bed.

"The way lies before you, Anna," the Spirit of Counsel said.

"Do not be seduced by what you see or what you hear," Chastity said. Just then, a bouquet of wonderful aromas greeted us. "Or what you smell," Chastity added with a laugh. We joined her.

"Thank you," I said to them sincerely—for it is not always the bad that seduces us; it is often the good (but not God's "good").

With that, they disappeared. Squaring my shoulders, I approached the group of flowers.

Talking to Flowers

As I walked up to them, an iris lifted her head and looked at me. "How did you get in here?"

"Now, Iris," said a petunia, "she probably has relatives here."

"Yes, Iris," joined in a yellow crocus, "you know no one gets through the gate unless they know someone important—well, I did not mean important..." The crocus stumbled over her words. "I mean a member."

"I'm sure she's fine," said a large pink tea rose sweetly.

"Oh, Rose," said the iris, "you are overblown with your own scent."

The iris turned to me. "Who are you, girl?"

"I'm Anna."

"Well?" asked the iris, as if expecting more.

"Don't crowd the child," said the petunia. "Give her time to catch her breath."

"I—I was brought here," I said, almost as a question.

The Boastful Pride of Life

"You see?" The petunia raised her head to better give the iris an I-told-you-so look.

"She has possibilities," chimed in a clump of daisies.

"Yes," agreed the petunia firmly.

"Oh, all this chitchat; let's just ask her," the hollyhock blossoms grumped. "Have you come for your petals?"

"I don't know," I stammered.

"Well, you cannot go further without your petals," the iris said firmly. All the flowers nodded in agreement.

"No one told me I needed petals to go further," I said.

"Typical!" barked the iris with a jerk of her head.

HIDDEN TEACHINGS

The tea rose whispered sympathetically, "It could be that she does not know because she is not advanced enough to receive the hidden teachings."

"Hidden teachings?"[1] I asked out loud.

"You see," interjected a tulip, "she doesn't even know what we mean. If you had asked me before this situation occurred…"

"What situation?" I asked.

"Miss Tulip, everything does not need to be OK'd by you. Your time of wrecking the economy of a country has passed," snapped a snapdragon.[2]

A WEED

"I'm just saying that she could be a weed," the tulip said haughtily.

---

1 Hidden teachings were part of many false doctrines such as the "Gnostic teachings." In the widest sense, the word means the belief in salvation by knowledge. The knowledge of self was primary—the self's true nature and the self's destiny. According to Gnostics, only a few attained to this self-knowledge, because only a few were selected to seek after it. They believe that if you know yourself, you will know that you are already sons of the living Father. You are born in the family of God with no need of salvation through Jesus. The Apocryphal gospels disclosed Jesus as divine principle. Jesus was not considered a real human being who lived a human life at a specific time in history according to Gnosticism.

2 According to Wikipedia, "Tulip mania was a period during the Dutch Golden Age when contract prices for some bulbs of the recently introduced and fashionable tulip reached extraordinarily high levels. The major acceleration started in 1634 and then collapsed in February 1637." At the mania's peak, just before the collapse, "some single tulip bulbs sold for more than 10 times the annual income of a skilled artisan." Some people sold their houses and farms to obtain a rare tulip bulb. ("Tulip mania," Wikipedia, accessed June 6, 2023, https://en.wikipedia.org/wiki/Tulip_mania#cite_note-2.)

"Oh no!" All the flowers cringed and shuddered.

"I'm not a weed," I said over the turmoil.

The iris retook charge: "Tulip is right. Pedigree matters."

"After all," the tulip said loftily, "we are in a bed with a Rothschild orchid."[3]

"And the Queen of the Night," sighed the tea rose worshipfully.

"What does she matter?" snapped the snapdragon. "She only blooms for a couple of hours once a year."[4]

"She needs her beauty sleep," soothed the rose.

"Nonsense," barked the snapdragon. "She's lazy." The flowers seemed to have forgotten that a human was in their midst.

The Need to Continue

"Excuse me," I said, "I believe I need to continue my journey—so..."

"Not without your petals," the iris said firmly.

The petunia tried to explain: "The path is long and sometimes tangled. With designer petals, you will always be treated as—well, you know—special."

---

3 Rothschild orchid—takes seven to ten years to mature, and the bloom may be two to three feet across. It is a graceful flower, with tall stems and strongly striped petals. Once open, Rothschild orchids can look like a flock of birds descending.

4 Queen of the Night—a species of cactus that rarely blooms. When it does bloom, it only blooms at night, and the flowers only last a few hours. It is native to Mexico and South America. Many consider it the most beautiful bloom in the world.

"They see the petals and know that you are one of us," the crocus purred with pride.

"Worthy of the light," the iris said imperiously.

The always soothing tea rose interjected to help the explanation: "With designer petals, you can always turn your face to the sun."

Answering the Flowers

"I don't mean to be disrespectful," I said, "but I can do that now."

"What are you saying?" all asked in shocked chorus.

"That I can turn to Jesus at any time," I answered.

"Oh." They nodded to one another. "Foundational teaching. We have gone beyond that."

The tulip continued: "With designer petals, you receive greater light—you are worthy of the secrets of the universe that have been reserved for a special, advanced few."

Nothing in the Word

"But there is nothing in the Word that says God gives special knowledge to only a few," I said.

"Ah," chuckled the iris, "now I see your difficulty." She nodded knowingly to the tulip. "The exclusive, and I must say, more advanced petals are found in other books—books that should have been part of the Bible, but politics kept them out. These other books have hidden secret knowledge."

"You can climb higher," trumpeted a trumpet vine.

"You have a spiritual pedigree with the right flowers... your bulbs are able to get into the most prestigious beds from preschool through college," the tea rose cooed as if seeking to convince another flower.

"You are much more powerful." The tulip lifted her head proudly. "Secret knowledge makes you powerful."

Is Power Our Purpose?

"But is power our purpose?" I asked.

"Certainly helps," the iris said, dismissing the question as unworthy of discussion. "Only those without power question power. When you have money, power, and even fame, you can"—it was as though she was trying to rethink the talking points that were mainly for flowers and reconstitute them for humans—"you can do so much more for people."

The tulip, seeing the iris struggling, joined in: "You can give others a hand up because you are traveling in the right circles. Your influence, of course, would be for good—always." All the flowers in the group smiled and nodded to one another.

"Like here," the iris continued. "We are bedded with some very famous flowers, and everyone wants to be us. The soil is enriched, and we are fertilized regularly. Therefore, all of us look wonderful." They all giggled like starlets that had received figure-enhancing surgery.

I smiled. "But ladies, looking wonderful is not the same as being wonderful," I said.

"Oh, don't be a nene,"[5] the snapdragon said sharply. "You know what we mean. If you have nothing and are no one, what good can you do?"

I paused a moment to contemplate what I had heard.

THE TWENTY-YEAR-OLD

I looked at these beautiful flowers and thought back to my twenty-year-old self when first I went to New York. I was dazzled by all the lights, activities, art galleries, famous and glamorous people. I would go to a bookstore and stand for long periods, looking at the pictures of famous actors and actresses—long dead. I began to think, even then, that all they had achieved and lived for was like vapor. No one remembered, and if anyone did remember, soon no one would be alive that admired their skill. It wasn't lasting. Even a brick in the bookstore wall lasted longer than their accomplishments.

Even then, unsaved and dedicated to embracing the world and all the pretty little lies of the world, a doubt was growing in me. "Why work to create something that will not last—like the work of the famous people in the photography books?"

I felt that I wanted to do something that would last. I wanted all the hard work to produce lasting rewards. But what?

5 Nene —a rare black-and-gray short-winged goose native to Hawaii.

Even though I was not a Christian at this time, I realized that everything in the world was passing away. One glance at the ruins of ancient civilizations told me that.

But what would last? People would say, "Oh, you live in their memories." But I did not want to live in order to be a memory for a few years in someone's psyche before that generation died. That was not enough.

I never found the answer until I came to Christ, and only then, after I had been a Christian for about twenty years, because when you are a new—a baby—Christian, you can be very fleshly. One must grow and mature in the spiritual life as one does in a regular human life on earth, because when the Lord first rescues us out of this world, we still see and do things as before, we still carry on trying to build in the world. Gradually we see this is also foolish. We get to the point where we only want to do and be and build what Jesus needs—and only if He asks us to accomplish that for Him on earth. Otherwise, we are living for the applause of humans, and applause dies fast.

But Jesus does tell us to store up treasures in heaven; well, that certainly is not gold, silver, or jewels. The streets in heaven are gold. It cannot be the glorious gifts the Lord has bestowed upon us. Well, no, these are His already. You might say He lends these to us to show forth His glory and to benefit the body of Christ.

What then? What lasts? What can be stored and remain and even be used later? The character of Christ.

His character is gained through our flesh being consigned to the cross on earth.

As we pick up our cross and move forward to serve Him, only the part of our soul that has been transformed into the likeness of Christ will carry over and remain. It took me years to not only understand that, but then to embrace and begin to live this truth, but always, always, only with Christ overcoming through me. For while I am in this mortal body, I will always need to take every thought captive to Christ.[6]

ADDRESSING THE FLOWERS

As I looked at the flowers, I realized that I pitied them. Therefore, I spoke gently to these beautiful, deluded blossoms rooted so firmly in the earth: "Jesus tells us, 'Do not love the world nor the things in the world. If anyone loves the world, the love of the Father is not in him. For all that is in the world, the lust of the flesh and the lust of the eyes and the boastful pride of life, is not from the Father, but is from the world. The world is passing away, and also its lusts; but the one who does the will of God lives forever.'"[7]

---

6 2 Corinthians 10:3–5 (NASB): "For though we walk in the flesh, we do not wage battle according to the flesh, for the weapons of our warfare are not of the flesh, but divinely powerful for the destruction of fortresses. We are destroying arguments and all arrogance raised against the knowledge of God, and we are taking every thought captive to the obedience of Christ."

7 1 John 2:15–17.

LEAVING THE GARDEN

Before they could answer, my breastplate tightened and I was sucked backward out of the garden, passing a sign that read: "Wind Tree."[8]

I could hear the clamor of "the ladies" arguing about my visit. The only expletive that rose above the others was, "A weed, if ever I saw one."

"No petals for her," I heard as I blew further and further away, tumbling toward the branches of the Wind Tree.

THE WIND TREE

The wind blew me through narrower and narrower passageways or branches. These were lined with some sort of mucus membranes and minute, tickling hairs that trapped dust and other harmful particles. I went tumbling and laughing through more constrictive branches until I came smashing into the thin walls of a tiny room.[9]

THE ROOM OF EXCHANGE

I felt a little like Alice in Wonderland when she ate a good deal of the "Eat Me" cake and grew too large to get from the anteroom into the garden. But I was also suspended,

---

8 The lungs

9 Alveoli: "the tiny air sacs at the end of the bronchioles....The alveoli are where the lungs and the blood exchange oxygen and carbon dioxide during the process of breathing in and out." ("Alveoli," National Cancer Institute, accessed June 6, 2023, https://www.cancer.gov/publications/dictionaries/cancer-terms/def/alveoli.)

by the force of the wind, to the walls of the small chamber—like an amusement park ride at the fair.

However, I was laughing so hard from the tumbling and tickling and being suspended in midair to the wall that I hardly felt the removal of all that was deleterious to me from the chambers of the corrupted heart. All passed right through the thin walls of that tiny room, and I felt clean and fresh amid this extraordinary experience. My heavenly Father's voice rattled the room's thin walls: "You have been given multiplied grace."[10]

Checkout Time

Instantly, the Holy Spirit filled me anew, and I was sucked out of the labyrinth of passageways into the chambers of the renewed heart and shot like a bottle rocket into the hallway. It seemed like an inglorious arrival, for my expulsion was rather like being spit out. I ended on my bottom with my legs out in front of me on the hallway's dirt floor.

Well Done

Ruach, Chastity, and the Spirit of Counsel clapped as I arrived.

"Well done," they said.

Ruach gave me a hand up.

The Spirit of Counsel said, "The breastplate has been

10 Grace can be multiplied as shown in 2 Peter 1:2: "Grace and peace be multiplied to you in the knowledge of God and of Jesus our Lord."

tested. But remember, 'Watch over your heart with all diligence, for from it flow the springs of life.'"[11]

"We must go, our friend," said the Spirit of Counsel.

"But be strong and courageous," said Chastity, smiling.

I hugged them both, and they bowed from the waist to Ruach and were gone.

Almost immediately, I heard the child cry again. "Help me. Please, help me!"

I turned to Ruach. "There it is again," I said. "Do you hear it?" We both listened but heard no more.

"Come on," I said to Ruach. "Let's see if we can find the one crying."

---

11 Proverbs 4:23.

Chapter 7

SHOES OF THE GOSPEL OF PEACE

SUDDENLY, I WAS sucked out past the tangled roots of the hallway and through two immense doors. The doors slammed behind me with impressive finality.

The Precipice

Immediately ahead of me, rocks thrust over a wide river of lava. Suffocating heat rolled over me. My breath was coming in jagged starts. My legs became rubbery, and I lost all strength in them. Panicked, I lowered myself carefully onto my hands and knees and inched backward until I could press my back against the safety of the two heavy doors.

It was only then that I realized that the lava flow was within an immense cavern. Shadows, like fingers, stretched up the cave walls, shifting with the boiling lava. Sweat was pouring from me—partly from the wilting heat and partly from stark fear. I was up high, and heights frightened me.

I thought: "Where is Ruach? I need Him to steady me."

At the door a sign read: "Change Shoes." When you cannot think of anything else, you can always follow directions. Mindlessly, I groped around for the shoes mentioned in the sign. The shoes were a pair of white ballet slippers. "Huh!" I said involuntarily and changed my shoes. The shoes from the sheepfold disappeared.

Suddenly, two spirits materialized near me. One was the outline of an older woman. Her hair was white and her garment puce. The other spirit looked to be about eight feet tall, with huge muscular arms and legs as large as small trees. He looked formidable to say the least—except that he appeared to be about fifteen years old. Both helpers, being spirit, slipped in and out of clear visibility.

Perhaps not so strangely, I began to feel agitated. Beyond my immediate surroundings, I could see a slender iron rod that crossed the boiling lava.

The older-looking spirit addressed me. "I am Patience," she said, putting her right hand over her heart, and this is Self-Control. Ruach asked us to accompany you across the River Ire.

"Ire," I choked. With every bit of courage I could muster, I rose to my hands and knees and crawled over to the beginning of the suspended rod. "It looks dangerous."

"It is dangerous if you are careless," Self-Control volunteered. It was unnerving that he was so casual.

"It looks dangerous even if I am not careless." I laughed painfully. I was, however, the only one laughing. Perhaps this was due to underlying resentment in my tone.

"All must pass over the River Ire," Self-Control added seriously.

"Do people fall off this rod?" I asked.

"Yes," Patience said, but she added no encouragement, like, "But you can do it." Instead, she piled discouragement on top of my fears. "The river boils with resentment, disillusionment, and vile hatred toward God and man."

As I stared down into that hellish crossing, she paused. Then, with a voice like a cattle prod, said, "You need to begin."

I sucked in a quick breath and steadied myself.

I knew I had to control myself. "With the Lord's help," I added.

And He did help me.

As I began to move from acting on raw emotions to using my brain, I thought, "Others have done this. It is not here to kill me but to help me. Anger at the process will do nothing. This must be doable."

I squared my shoulders and shakily slid my right foot onto the thin iron rod. It was warm from the lava flow below. I mumbled under my breath, "Lord, help me."

Generally, I am not of the temperament that becomes angry. I had found that there are a couple of seconds after one is insulted that the emotions pass the insult on to the brain, and the emotions allow the brain to either react negatively against the insult or decide to let it pass. For years now, I have just let the insult pass. But there was something in this test that was pushing me beyond my usual, casual release of the prods. I held my breath and hoped the shoes were good for something like tightrope walking.

I, like most people, have no training in this type of balancing act. So I tried to remember every picture of tightrope walkers I had ever seen: arms out, adjusting balance, all of it.

However, even as I inched across the River Ire, not only fear but anger shot through me like electricity. I felt that I should not have been put into this dangerous position. My face flushed, and my hands shook. Actually, I think I slipped into a mild shock, for it had been many years since I had experienced such raw fear and accompanying resentment. But suddenly I was bombarded with both.

"Breathe," I told myself. But I could not concentrate on breathing. With every bit of self-control, I tried to move my thinking away from old offenses—even those against God. But my emotions were unstable—they were rather like the ball in a pinball machine pinging from one emotion to another. I did regain my awareness enough to tell myself that I might be under attack. Then it came to me that such an attack might be coming from the fumes rising from below.

"Well, demons can be contained," I said to myself. Out loud, I said, "Leave me, in Jesus name." The fumes dispersed quickly, but they left me with a bitter aftertaste in my mouth.

"So it was demons," I said to myself.

OTHERS WITHIN THE CAVE

Out of the corner of my eye, I could see many other people struggling to cross their own rods. Angels flew with them as Patience and Self-Control were flying with me.

Noticing others engaged in the same struggle gave me courage. If they could do this, then so could I.

TERROR

Suddenly, I heard a blood-curdling scream. I froze on the metal rod. Someone was falling. I listened to the long fall of the terrorized person—screaming all the way down. "That could have been me," I thought. The thought paralyzed me.

Patience asked an uncharacteristic question: "Do you think this is unfair?"

"Yes," I choked with spontaneous honesty. Almost as quickly I breathed out "No!" I did not want to let my thinking drop into accusations. I thought of Job's friends who were urging him to curse God and die. It was too easy to accuse. I had to get my thinking straight. "God is always fair," I told myself. "I can't always see it, but I know Him, and I trust Him. I—I love Him."

In a dry whisper I said, "Resentment and anger are never the answers." Saying this in some way soothed my heart, which seemed to be hardening. I continued: "We are on earth to represent the Prince of Peace. If you love someone, you trust them. I am here because I trust God," I said to myself.

I was growing stronger as I spoke.

"With the Lord's help I am going forward." I gritted my teeth, and with sweat pouring from my face, I slid my foot forward on the rod. It wasn't walking so much as sliding my foot forward and then dragging the other to meet it.

THE DOGS OF WAR

Suddenly, vicious dogs rushed to the edge of several protruding rocks, trying to leap high enough to bite me. They startled and shook me. I swayed dangerously over the molten Ire.

"Steady," whispered Self-Control. "Do not let the unbelievers frighten you."

"Keep your eyes on Christ," Patience added.

Self-Control continued to coach me: "Let Christ within you master your fear."

I asked within, "How do I do that? Perhaps I do harbor bitterness against unbelievers that persecute me. I know I bristle inside, but I am trying to let Christ remove all hardness of heart from me."

I continued to speak internally: "I want to forgive the wrongs done to me. If those who attack me are unsaved, they are like the walking dead and do not understand.

If believers, then who knows where they are in growing up into the likeness of Christ. They could be spiritual babies—or teenagers who still feel the pull of the world's illusions. Who knows where anyone is on the road to allowing Christ to replace their fleshly soul with Himself?"

Even as the dogs continued snapping at me, they were joined by the roar of lions perilously near me on the rod.

THE LIONS OF WRATH

A very angry man roared behind me, "Get going! Who do you think you are?"

Another, further behind me on the rod, countered: "Leave her alone. Do you want her to fall?"

Being unfairly attacked by those who were obviously believers—for they were walking the same path—rattled me. We were all doing our best to cross the lava.

"Stop!" I cried out in panic. I flung my arms out wildly, trying to keep my balance.

"I'll stop when you move it," the voice behind me roared. "Go on!"

Fury leaped on me like wild beasts. Blood rushed to my face, scalding my eyes.

"No! Stop!" both spirits cried. It was difficult because such wrath dug in deeper because believers are family. It hurts more.

Then Self-Control whispered in my ear, "Stop and think." The spirit was right. I was rushing into the temporary madness of anger. Was I not old enough in the Lord to be past all of this? Suddenly, like Paul, I was confronted with the ever-present flesh. Like Paul, I cried out to God, "Will I never be free from this flesh?"

"No," said Patience calmly, "not as long as you are in your body. But," she added, "the lack of character in others does not excuse the lack of character in you."

"Lack of character," I said, as if deflating a balloon. There it was. I had let my emotions drive me into the flesh. I was weary. "Help me," I whispered.

"Do as your Lord," said Self-Control. "Take the unrighteous blows as He did for your sake. Vengeance belongs to God." The truth from God's Word pierced my heart. I forced a deep sigh, letting the knot of anger unravel. After a time of silence, I said, "O God, forgive me. Let me live in peace with You and mankind." Asking for forgiveness seemed to help. Slowly the sting from this verbal attack began to ease. Also, my mind began to clear, and the beasts and the dogs backed away.

Amazingly, releasing this anger and asking the Lord to help me so unexpectedly buoyed me that I became positively giddy. I sang out, "Let me live as You have said in Your Word: 'All of you be harmonious, sympathetic, brotherly, kindhearted, and humble in spirit; not returning evil for evil or insult for insult, but giving a blessing instead; for you were called for the very purpose that you might inherit a blessing.'[1] As it is better that I suffer for

1 1 Peter 3:8–9.

doing what is right, if You should choose, Lord, than if I do that which is wrong."

The End in Sight

Oh, praise God, the end was in sight. Suddenly, the fear of the Lord came upon me, for I remembered Moses, who took all manner of abuse for forty years while guiding the children of Israel through the desert, only to strike the Rock in anger and thereby disqualify himself from entering the Promised Land right at the end.

"God, help me," I said. "I don't want to have come this far and lose the prize right at the end."

Leaving

I practically leaped to the solid ground on the far side. I turned to look back at the lava flow. I was sweaty, but I had made it. I had made it! I knew I had passed the test. Suddenly, special armored boots covered the slippers.

"Thank You, Lord," I sighed, smiling.

Almost immediately, the two spirits and I flew through the opened door of the cavern into the root-clogged hallway.

Ruach greeted us all: "Well done, Anna," He said, "and friends." The two angels seemed wonderfully jovial. We were all a little giddy.

"We will leave you here," said Patience and Self-Control, bowing.

"We have been assigned to you, Anna," said Patience,

smiling and looking amazingly younger with the weight of the ordeal behind us.

"Therefore, we will see you later," said a strangely more mature-looking Self-Control, smiling.

"Thank you, dear friends." I hugged them exuberantly, leaving them somewhat gobsmacked. They smiled sheepishly toward me, then bowed to Ruach and vanished before I had the chance to think through their transformations.

Suddenly, I heard that child cry again. I turned my face in that direction, and my body followed. "Ruach," I said, "we're closer."

Chapter 8

THE SHIELD OF FAITH

I FOLLOWED THE SOUND of the child crying until it ceased, and I was left standing in the root-tangled hallway. When my focus narrowed to my own surroundings, I saw that the light had changed. The passageway had once been brighter. However, as I traveled deeper into this root system, the hallways were becoming darker and darker.

A Car Named Decisions

Without warning, I heard the rattle of something on tracks. Then, almost immediately, several linked steel cars rounded a corner. They rattled from side to side, sort of like old roller-coaster rides, and stopped near me. The paint was peeling from the dented compartments, and the once shiny plastic seats were now gummy and torn. I saw the name "Decisions" on the grimy hood of the lead car.

The cars stopped before the entrance to a large root. Prominently displayed over the door were the words "The Swill."

Ruach appeared and spoke tensely: "Prepare your shield."

I looked toward the area that would have been His face, if I could have seen it.

"What is swill?" I whispered.

"It is the canker that eats the heart as the mind and spirit battle for ascendency. Prepare your shield," He reiterated.

I thought, "I don't understand." While trying to work out the reply in my mind, I rotated the shield from the location across my back, where I had stashed it. Finally, my curiosity got the better of me. I half blurted out: "I'm sorry," I said. "What is swill?"

Ruach helped me fit the shield onto my left arm as He answered: "It is the slop fed to hogs." His answer stunned me.

THE ARRIVAL OF KNOWLEDGE

Suddenly, another angel appeared near the waiting coaster ride.

Ruach welcomed him in a low voice: "Knowledge."

The angel was tall and noble in countenance. He wore a garment covered in Bible verses. I also noticed that he wore chest-high wader boots with a good deal of his garment stuffed into the top—under his suspenders.

"May I join you?" He smiled but spoke in equally low tones.

"Please," I answered. Then I caught my error in protocol. "I mean, if it's alright with You," I asked Ruach.

"More than alright," He affirmed, "for Knowledge

has been assigned to accompany you." Ruach took my right hand to assist me into the nearest compartment. "Knowledge, this is our Anna."

Knowledge bowed at the waist. I tried to do the same (which does not work as well when climbing into a narrow compartment).

"Please," Ruach said as He gestured for Knowledge to climb into the compartment near me. Knowledge obliged.

"I am pleased to be here." He smiled as he sat down.

"Wait," I whispered, "where is your shield?"

"I'm getting behind yours." He smiled.

I choked a laugh. "Well, that's good to know."

The car lurched and then began to move forward. I was as excited as if going on a roller-coaster ride. "We're going!" I turned, smiling toward Ruach, who was being left behind.

"Remember your shield," He called tensely.

I held up my shield, but His words dampened my momentary lightheartedness.

From Above

We bumped through a couple of padded double doors into an inky half-light...the sort that somewhat conceals the scary pop-ups in carnival sideshows.

"Lift your shield, Anna," Knowledge urged. I had just lifted it when two fiery darts hit it and bounced off. "Just in time," he laughed. "That was Despair and Guilt."

"They are on fire!" I blurted out in alarm.

"No one said that they would play fair," Knowledge said with a smile.

"But who would shoot at us?" I asked as more and more fiery darts bounced off the shield.

"Former friends," Knowledge said, ducking behind the shield.

"Friends?"

"Demons," was his blunt answer. "They once desired the things of God, but when they turned, it was not just a little; instead, they deliberately stood against all they once supported. Now they not only oppose God having His desires, but hinder others from serving Him. There is no one more vicious than one who was once for God's purposes and then turns to stand against Him."

Hopelessness

All of a sudden, we dipped and began to sink. "Wait a minute!" I cried out involuntarily.

"Lift your shield!" Knowledge shouted.

"But we're sinking," I blurted out. Honestly, I could not see why lifting my shield would help. Maybe we could use it as a paddle. I could see now why Knowledge wore chest-high waders. But all I could do was follow instructions. I lifted my shield high just as the arrows named Disbelief, Distrust, and Doubt drove deep into the plastic seats, trying to attack the shield of faith.

"Whew!" Knowledge exhaled after being missed by such lethal projectiles. I pulled them out and extinguished their fire in the surrounding goo even as we sort of bumped down another notch into the putrid soup.

I thought to myself, "I'm thankful I can swim."

We were bombarded suddenly by dozens of arrows—too many to read. Creeping fear sent a chill through me as a javelin by that name hit the shield and thudded off into the swill. Slowly, we were sinking up to our waists in the garbage. Severed human hands and animal parts floated on the surface. The stench was dreadful.

IN THE GOO

I could see many people struggling in this swamp of Swill. Some were having difficulty keeping their heads above the slop, and some were clinging to their partially submerged roller-coaster cars, thinking those could save them. Within the swill were Berkshire hogs having the time of their lives. These hogs had enormous ears.[1] (I supposed that they were the reason we were whispering before the ride began.)

On the bank, dozens of these massive swine were luxuriating half in and half out of their scrounged holes.

Hopelessness began to hang in the air like a black cloud.

I saw other hogs with nets that they were throwing into the slop to catch people as though they were fish. The people were trying to stay afloat, but there seemed to be little resistance to being caught. It looked more

---

1 Berkshire hogs are stocky with six white markings: four white "socks," a white snout, and white markings in the tail area. They have extremely large ears that are turned forward on their heads.

like coping on their part...reasoning their way into some sort of mental acceptance. Sometimes it seems that if we get dragged down low enough, we join forces with our captors: some kind of spiritual Stockholm syndrome.

REVELATION

"That's what it is," I confirmed within myself. "They don't believe God will save them. They have lost faith." I was reinforced in this revelation as I saw many trying to eat the slop right along with the pigs. Just then the gears on our car clogged, and we stopped.

"The swill," I shouted to Knowledge. "The swill is Unbelief!"

I was so stunned by this revelation that I missed two flaming arrows that sank deep into the top of the plastic seats. Knowledge grabbed them. They were little ones—Wavering and Misgivings—but they were burning quite a hole in the plastic.

"Trust in God, Anna," shouted Knowledge as suddenly he was being swept away but was still clamoring to help me. "Remember," he cried, "he who comes to God must believe that He is...and..."

I could see that I could not reach him, but I wanted to encourage him, so I called back: "And He is a rewarder of those who seek Him," I chimed in, completing the phrase.[2]

---

2 Hebrews 11:6: "And without faith it is impossible to please Him, for he who comes to God must believe that He is and that He is a rewarder of those who seek Him."

Knowledge called from even further away, "God never abandons those who fight for His cause."[3]

"Trust in Him alone," he called loudly, from an even greater distance. And he was gone.

"What is the matter with me?" I thought. "That's what I need to do, cry for help." I cried out, "Help me, Lord!"

"Help, Lord," I shouted again. "I'm sinking!" I began to talk to myself frantically: "Remember, His desire to save me is greater than anyone's desire to destroy me." I began to build myself up on my most holy faith.[4] I remembered that when Peter walked on water toward the Lord and began to sink, he cried out to the Lord, who immediately saved him.[5]

Others in the swill began to cry out in the gall of their bitterness, for they were trying to extract themselves in their own strength.

"Lord, help!" I cried louder. But He did not answer. He answered Peter but not me. And I could no longer see my traveling companion, Knowledge.

---

3 Deuteronomy 31:6: "Be strong and courageous, do not be afraid or tremble at them, for the LORD your God is the one who goes with you. He will not fail you or forsake you."

4 Jude 20: "But you, beloved, building yourselves up on your most holy faith, praying in the Holy Spirit..."

5 Matthew 14:30–31 (NASB): "But seeing the wind, he became frightened, and when he began to sink, he cried out, saying, 'Lord, save me!' Immediately Jesus reached out with His hand and took hold of him, and said to him, 'You of little faith, why did you doubt?'"

From Below

Something from within the Swill began wrapping around me and pulling me down. I kicked at it. I could feel suction cups, like tentacles, attaching to my body.

"Why doesn't the Lord help me?" I asked myself, panicking. "And where is Knowledge?" There is a point when even the most faith-filled child of God feels so overwhelmed that he begins to lose heart. I was so discouraged. I could feel myself letting go.

I slipped into a stunned melancholy. I was going down and began to justify letting go. I was seeking salvation from the only One who could give it. I believed He would rescue me. But where was He?

I began to sink to a depth to which I was unaccustomed. Generally, if sad, I did not drop further and further from the light into a black funk of depression. But now I began to slip stonily into self-pity. I felt myself being pulled under, but I was so disimpassioned by the struggle that I justified my actions. "Why fight it?" I wondered. "Perhaps surrender would be peaceful." I thought I might as well give up and let it take me under—I felt so overwhelmed.

The Lifeline of Memories-

Softly, I began to resist less. With less resistance, I slid deeper into the Swill. Strangely, as I sank, a story Bob Jones (a prophetic minister) told me flashed into my mind.

Bob grew up in the mountains of Arkansas among people that held bitter grudges and often took violent revenge. He told me that while in the VA hospital, before he was saved, he planned to sneak out at night and cause terminal harm to several people against whom his family sought revenge.

Afterward, he calculated, he would sneak back in before dawn, thereby giving himself an air-tight alibi. However, before he could put this plan into action, Jesus Christ appeared to him in his hospital room and stopped him. After Bob repented and accepted Christ as his Lord and Savior, the Lord spoke to him in the vernacular of the Arkansas mountains, saying: "I do not want to see you wallow in self-pity ever again," and Bob didn't. The Lord told him that self-pity led to the feeling of victimization, and victimization led to bitterness, and a root of bitterness led to retaliation.

While sinking, the Lord brought that story back to my mind because that was exactly what I was doing; I, like the hogs, was beginning to wallow.

Self-pity was dragging me down into depression, and depression—like a many-tentacled octopus—was pulling me down into black despair and unbelief.

GRACE

Suddenly, God Almighty stirred within me. He gave me abounding grace.[6] It was like light in the darkness. Grace

6 Romans 5:20: "But where sin increased, grace abounded all the more." God displays His abounding grace through His love. We know He will always do what is best for His children. He not only brings them to Himself by extending grace to them, but He continues to increase grace to them through sanctification—transforming them into His likeness.

gave me the power to change my decisions. Immediately I was so shot through with hope and faith that it seemed to me that I was in no peril at all. I tingled with expectancy. I shouted into the void: "Blessed Lord, You are the One who saves Your own. You love me and will not allow your beloved to see corruption.[7] 'I know that my Redeemer lives...whom my eyes will see, and not another,'" I burst forth in exuberance.[8]

"I know You, Lord. I know Your promises, and I know Your heart. We are in covenant, Daddy, sealed in the blood of Your only begotten Son, Jesus. I will not fear for I am already seated with You in heavenly places.[9] You will deliver me from this trial. But even if You do not deliver me, let it be known that I will not serve another god. I will serve You alone, my Redeemer and my King."

Knowledge appeared and grabbed the half-submerged shield and pulled. I was hanging onto the shield, and miraculously the roller-coaster ride also began to surface from the slop and vomit.

People floundering in the goo shouted and cried abuses at me as I was being airlifted out.

PASSING THE TEST

A loud ping rang from the shield.

---

7 Psalm 16:10 (NASB): "For You will not abandon my soul to Sheol; You will not allow Your Holy One to undergo decay."

8 Job 19:25, 27 (NASB): "Yet as for me, I know that my Redeemer lives...whom my eyes will see, and not another."

9 Ephesians 2:6: "And raised us up with Him, and seated us with Him in the heavenly places in Christ Jesus..."

Suddenly, I and the car passed through some sort of "car wash." Water sprayed from all sides—taking my breath away. Then blowers nearly pulled out my hair, drying me off!

Out

Out I went through padded swinging doors again into the hallway. I was clean, and even the coaster car looked new. Looking at the front of the hood upside down, I could see a word had been uncovered from the gummy dirt which had hidden it before we went through the wash. The car hood now read "Faithful Decisions" emblazoned in gold. Everything looked so new.

Distantly, I could hear the multitude of people in the Swill of unbelief crying out. Some had begun to cry out for the Lord—which was encouraging. Some were railing in the hog wallow of bitterness from which I had been supernaturally removed.

The cars came to a halt amid the tangled roots. Knowledge walked out through the padded swinging doors with a broad smile on his face.

"Knowledge!" Ruach exclaimed with joy.

"She did well," Knowledge said, continuing to smile.

"Thank you." I reached out to shake his hand as he passed.

He looked down at my hand, puzzled. (This is obviously not a custom in heaven.)

"Thank you," I said as I grabbed his hand to shake it in a way that said, "This is a way we thank others."

He caught on and shook my hand vigorously.

"You will see Knowledge again," Ruach said.

"Yes, you will—but now I must leave you. The great King be with you." Knowledge bowed at the waist to Ruach and smiled at me as he left.

I started to peek at my Father's mantle but decided to wait.

Chapter 9

THE HELMET OF SALVATION

As Ruach and I made our way downward, the hall became more and more choked with roots of every size. These were tangled and snarled on the floor and on the walls. Roots now were hanging from the dirt ceiling—dangling down in a loose, though claustrophobic curtain.

A tall, warm-looking angel appeared near the mouth of the next root. Ruach called to her: "We're here. Don't leave without Anna."

"No, I won't," she said, laughing.

He turned to me: "This is Wisdom."

It was difficult to tell if she was old or young—maybe both. Her blazing red hair showed glints of silver. It was piled on top of her head with a golden tiara securing the intricate hair design. She was straight as an arrow with golden sandals partially seen beneath her draped, loose-fitting garment. Coils of gold crisscrossed her chest.

"Welcome, Anna," Wisdom said with a smile. "Are you ready for the helmet to be tested?"

"With the Lord's help," I answered. She smiled. Then I added softly, "Thank you for going with me."

She touched my cheek with her fingertips: "Of course, dear child."

Ruach interjected, "Put on your helmet, Anna. There is no time to waste."

Robotically, I did as He said. I felt a mixture of excitement and trepidation with a tinge of breathless urgency because we were near the end of the testing and closer to engaging whatever needed to be confronted in order to release the beneficence that the body of Christ needed in the last days.

I looked at Wisdom and tried to speak with confidence: "I'm ready!" Then to Ruach I added, "Thank you, Ruach." I made a decisive pivot to the mouth of the cave-like root.

Wisdom smiled indulgently and led the way. We entered the tunnel.

THE DITCH

Upon entering, there were high puttylike walls on either side of a steep cavern.[1] We began walking a narrow path at the bottom.

1 "The folds in the brain are called gyri, and the grooves are called sulci. These morphological features are produced by the folding of the cortex, the part of our brain responsible for higher cognitive processes like memories, language, and consciousness...While neuronal cells grow and divide, the increasingly bigger brain leads to a compression of the cortex and the forming

"It's very dark here," I said to Wisdom.

"Yes," she replied. "This is the Ditch of Unreasonable Thinking."

"Unreasonable?" I half laughed.

"Yes, those who come to Christ are particularly susceptible to walking into this ditch."

"But why?" I asked.

"Because when they come to Christ, His love floods their hearts, and they equate the change in their lives to include the outer world around them. They expect life on earth to be easier from then on."

I blanched.

Wisdom laughed: "I see you have fallen prey to equating Christianity with fantasy."

"I did, I must confess."

"And what helped you?" she asked

"I suppose I grew up. I realized that if the Son of God was persecuted on earth—and He was perfect—who was I to escape?"

The Orchard of Thoughts

There was a greater light up ahead, but I could hear the sizzle of exposed electricity—which was alarming. However, Wisdom was leading us upward. We quickly arrived in a stunningly beautiful orchard filled with—what seemed to be—electric trees. Light and power

---

of folds." ("Question of the Week: Why do brains have wrinkles?," University College London, April 27, 2017, https://tinyurl.com/mr26dwjf.)

were flashing and crackling from tree to tree so that the orchard actually seemed to sing. It was beautiful.[2]

"When you live in harmony with the Holy One, it is as if these trees clap their hands and sing praises to the Lord," Wisdom said.

We began walking through the trees as she spoke. It felt invigorating there.

Suddenly, buckshot pellets began to hit my helmet.

"What?" I exclaimed.

"Guard yourself, Anna," Wisdom said.

I raised my hand to shield my eyes as I looked up to ascertain the direction of the pellets. I saw a blackened tree. Its branches were shriveled, and many limbs were broken. It sat in a black hole with what looked to be festering materials around it.

"Toxic thoughts, Anna," she whispered.

"What?" I gasped.

"The mangled and withered trees come from snarled, negative thoughts such as anger and resentment," she said. "These attract demons."

Then I saw the culprits.

Small, frightening demons were clustered around the black hole, chunking rocks at me. A couple of demons were cutting around the jagged edge of the opening with knives and then eating the corrupted flesh. They were looking at me and laughing.

---

2 These are neurons, information messengers in the brain that use electrical impulses and chemical signals to transmit information to the rest of the nervous system.

The whole area stank.

"The smell is dreadful," I said.

"The skull keeps most people from having to smell this rot. But it's there." Wisdom turned to me: "Negative thoughts are poisonous to those created to hold the Spirit of God. But the enemy finds many who are angry, and He goads them into dark corners. Once trapped, he tortures them into bitterness—which eventually will destroy them."[3]

"But how?" I asked.

"Not only because it blocks God's life from flowing to them, but toxic thoughts make cells in their body porous so that viruses can slip in and make the person ill. But the children of God do not need to cooperate with the evil one—letting him lead them around by the nose. They have the helmet of salvation. Our Lord has raised them up from the death walk of being a slave to Satan, to newness of life. The enemy no longer controls them. Now they may take every thought captive to Christ.[4] Now they do not need to ruminate upon every thought the enemy jams into their mind."

---

3 Negative thoughts: studies have found that "prolonged negative thinking diminishes your brain's ability to think, reason, and form memories." (Terry Small, "Is Negative Thinking Bad for Your Brain?" Chartered Professional Accountants of British Columbia, November 7, 2018, https://www.bccpa.ca/news-events/latest-news/2018/is-negative-thinking-bad-for-your-brain.

4 Take every thought captive to Christ: 2 Corinthians 10:3–5 (NASB): "For though we walk in the flesh, we do not wage battle according to the flesh, for the weapons of our warfare are not of the flesh, but divinely powerful for the destruction of fortresses. We are destroying arguments and all arrogance raised against the knowledge of God, and we are taking every thought captive to the obedience of Christ."

Wild Horses

Suddenly, the area where we were standing began to rumble. I braced myself against the side of a nearby high cliff's wall.

Wisdom leaned over to make sure I heard her: "Step back into this recess, Anna." She spoke loudly because the thundering of horses' hooves and screaming riders were upon us. Almost immediately they were thundering past us.

There were hundreds of wild horses. Fierce black demons were mounted on a few and driving the others. They called out and cracked long whips over the animals.

"This is what happens when emotions run your thinking," Wisdom said loudly. "You often have stampedes."

I was equally as loud: "This is dangerous."

The horses were crashing up against the sides of the high-walled cavern, causing gut-wrenching damage. I knew this would cause disastrous damage to the cells, compromising the walls.

"How do we stop them?" I shouted.

"Call for help," she shouted back.

"Help, Lord!" I called out as loudly as I could shout.

Immediately scores of spirits that looked like white whisps swooped in and mounted the rampaging steeds. Almost as quickly, one of the "wranglers" scooped me up and plunked me onto the back of a stampeding horse. I was petrified; I grabbed a handful of the horse's mane and lay down with my other arm and hand around its neck. I was hanging on for dear life. The ride was wilder than the horse itself, for I was jerked and jostled as we thundered down the narrow cavern. The ghostly riders bellowed and whooped with joy as they sought to turn the stampede into a cul-de-sac in order to corral them.

Frantically, I sought an answer to runaway emotions. Panic drove my brain to sort through my mental archives at record speed. I came across 2 Peter 1:5–6 (CSB): "For this very reason, make every effort to supplement your faith with goodness, goodness with knowledge, knowledge with self-control." I always wondered why self-control was a fruit of the Holy Spirit. Now I knew.

Because I had the Holy Spirit, I had self-control. I just needed to apply it. I reined in my emotions.

Amazingly, the ghostly wranglers were able to turn the lead horse into the large cul-de-sac. Therefore, the horses, though highly charged, began to settle down eventually and then simply milled around.

I waited a few seconds to settle myself also. There was an occasional neigh or toss of the head, but for the most part the horses were now quiet and docile. That was probably the reason the whisp-like spirits silently dissipated.

I waited a couple of minutes more, drawing in deep breaths. Finally, with a long sigh of relief, I slid from the horse's back. I stood, patting the steed, and looked around. The cul-de-sac was honeycombed with ancient-looking fortresses carved into its high walls. These recessed structures seemed to be abandoned. They had been active and populated earlier in someone's life with embittered stress—but now the Lord had cleaned them out. Therefore, the horses, now calm, milled their way back into the narrow corridor.

Wisdom appeared

"What is this place?" I asked.

"Abandoned fortresses," she said, "where past anger or hostility or resentment carved these strongholds into canyon walls. Hate, you see, requires more and more room to spread out and grow. It also produces thorns on the memory trees and hardens people into unforgiveness."

"But these are clean now?" I wondered.

"Yes, oh yes. These caves have not been visited for years."

"Is it safe to explore them?"

"Of course." Wisdom nodded.

I gave the horse that had carried me a couple of final pats and left him. Then, weaving through the rest of the tired horses, we made our way to the recessed structures. Upon entering one of the strongholds, the air was cool and dry. The walls were black as if at one time they had been tarred. Little light shone within. But still, on the floor was a sticky black sludge. This made walking precarious. Wisdom seemed to float above it.

"What is this?" I asked.

"Toxic waste. Be careful not to fall into it. This waste builds up within the cells from unforgiveness and bitterness. It makes the cells sticky until there are blockages. This sludge is a residue. It's still being cleared."

"But how?"

"Forgiveness. Your Lord and Savior shed His blood and died on the cross to give you this gift of forgiveness. The least the child of God can do is to pass this forgiveness on to others. The Word says: 'In everything give thanks; for this is the will of God.'[5] This is not optional, it is a command, Anna. As the child of God obeys, the Lord replaces sullen and dark memories with powerful, joyous thoughts."

We began climbing the stairs to an abandoned tower. I was mulling over what Wisdom had said. Finally, I answered her as honestly as I could: "I always want to forgive, but at times I do not feel it."

"Ah," she said with a smile. "That is the problem, isn't it? You may believe the Word is true, but try as you might, you are unable to turn your emotions."

"Yes," I agreed.

"Then," she continued, "you must lean on the Lord through His Word."

We arrived at the top of the tower, and I looked out. Different areas of this internal landscape spread out before me. I thought to myself that this was truly a complex control center, vital to our Lord and to His work on earth. Struggling, I prayed within myself, hoping that the Lord would line up my thinking with the mind of Christ.

"Come, Anna," Wisdom urged after we fully scanned

5 1 Thessalonians 5:18.

the area. She continued her explanation as we navigated the narrow stairway down.

Wisdom continued: "The Lord asks for humility on your part. All humans are being tested on earth, Anna. This is the reason He asks, 'Who are you to judge the servant of another? To his own master he stands or falls.'[6] That person's life is none of your business, frankly.

"You do have a job here on earth, and that is to allow the Holy Spirit to mature you in the Lord so that you, like your Master, forgive everyone from your heart. The Word says this, 'If each of you does not forgive his brother from your heart.'"[7]

We were outside of the abandoned stronghold again. It was eerily quiet now that the hundreds of horses had dwindled away.

Wisdom smiled at me—that sort of warm, motherly smile—reassuring in the circumstance.

"I will meet you outside, Anna." She stopped and looked back at me. "Speak from your heart, for the heart is the final judge within."

She disappeared. Just as quickly, I found myself before a panel of Elders. I supposed that is what they were. These were not dressed in white—but black. I was trying to count them quickly but could not. Each black-robed

---

6 Romans 14:4: "Who are you to judge the servant of another? To his own master he stands or falls; and he will stand, for the Lord is able to make him stand."

7 Matthew 18:35: "My heavenly Father will also do the same to you, if each of you does not forgive his brother from your heart."

justice was seated behind a high bench. Immediately, I realized I had come to the final test.

"Anna," the chief justice intoned.

I swallowed hard.

"Are you here to give answer?"

"I am."

"Will you abide by our judgment?"

"I will."

"Then so be it," the chief justice intoned loudly. "In the ancient texts there is no mention of a conscience. Without mentioning that which today is felt to be extremely important, is conscience just an invention of mankind's imagination?"

I closed my eyes and said internally. "Lord, please help me. Give me not only grace but abounding grace." I opened my eyes and squared my shoulders as I spoke.

Answering

"Conscience may not be called by that particular name in the Torah, but it is the first and most decisive reality shown in the Word. Adam and Eve hid after they had sinned. They were ashamed because their conscience convicted them even before the Lord condemned their actions.[8] Jacob's sons

---

8 Genesis 3:4–8 (NASB): "The serpent said to the woman, 'You certainly will not die! For God knows that on the day you eat from it your eyes will be opened, and you will become like God, knowing good and evil.' When the woman saw that the tree was good for food, and that it was a delight to the eyes, and that the tree was desirable to make one wise, she took some of its fruit and ate; and she also gave some to her husband with her, and he ate. Then the eyes of both of them were opened, and they knew that they were naked; and they sewed fig leaves together and made themselves waist coverings. Now they heard the

were ashamed for what they did to their brother, Joseph.[9] King David's heart staggered and stumbled because he had shed Uriah's blood without cause.[10]

"Our God provides a final checkpoint in the heart to help us live the life a child of God is called to live. For the Word says, 'Beloved, if our heart does not condemn us, we have confidence before God.'[11]

"The Torah may not have given us the word *conscience*, but it revealed the seat of this final arbitrator within the heart."

There was a pause. The Elders broke into smiles. "The answer has been given."

"Your armor is now fully tested, Anna. Unsheathe your sword."

LIFTING THE SWORD

I pulled the sword out of its sheath. It was gleaming and now had scripture all over it—scripture that seemed to change from time to time. I thought that the Scripture references probably changed as needed.

"You have received this sword from your Father in

---

sound of the LORD God walking in the garden in the cool of the day, and the man and his wife hid themselves from the presence of the LORD God among the trees of the garden."

9 Genesis 37:29: "Now Reuben returned to the pit, and behold, Joseph was not in the pit; so he tore his garments."

10 2 Samuel 12:13: "Then David said to Nathan, 'I have sinned against the LORD.' And Nathan said to David, 'The LORD also has taken away your sin; you shall not die.'"

11 1 John 3:21: "Beloved, if our heart does not condemn us, we have confidence before God."

order that you may fight the good fight for Christ crucified and lift up His standard for all to see."

Faster than lightning, I was removed from the testing ground. Immediately I was in the root cave hall again. Ruach and Wisdom awaited me.

Wisdom spoke: "Your heavenly Father has extended might to you, Anna. This is not earned but freely given from His heart and hand."

Ruach continued: "Your armor has been tested, Anna."

"Thank you, friends, for your support and help. I bless you in the name of the Lord. I will hasten to the job at hand."

"You aren't too fatigued to begin right away?" Wisdom asked.

"No, invigorated," I answered. And indeed, I was flushed with the excitement of the armor having been tested, and, I suppose, having been tested myself right along with it.

"Go with God, Anna. May He give you stunning victory for all our sakes." Wisdom disappeared.

Chapter 10

THE DEATH ADDER[1]

THERE WAS NO time to wait. I checked my sword and armor and then looked at Ruach.

"Where?" I asked.

Ruach silently pointed toward a dim light ahead. Immediately I moved forward. "Pray for me, Ruach!" I called over my shoulder.

Entering

The root system had narrowed, and the earth closed around the one way into the lighted area. My hearing became more acute as I took a cautious step toward the only avenue left for advancing. The hanging roots were now plastered against the narrowing entrance walls due to a suction pulling both them and me nearer the light. The sound of a deep drum kept a constant, dull beat in the background. It was frightening, truly ominous. I did not know where it came from and could not stop it.

1 Satan does not have the ability to be in multiple places at the same time, as does Christ. God is omnipresent. Therefore, this is one of Satan's workers assigned to guard this important acquisition of the satanic kingdom.

Where was I going? The walls narrowed to a crawl space. That too was frightening. What if something began crawling on me or stinging me? I couldn't defend myself. I remembered the taunt that only the meek could find this beneficence. Well, I was certainly down on my knees. The suction became greater. I was getting closer, and my fear was growing right along with the nearness to the opening.

I began to pray out loud—"Yea, though I walk through the valley of the shadow of death..."[2]

The drum stopped and everything was deathly still. I tried to keep my movements as well as my breath from making sounds. I didn't know what was up ahead. I knew my Father would not have given me *might* if I did not need it. But I didn't feel mighty.

Ruach seemed to have disappeared, and I was nearer and nearer danger. Through all the trials and the tests, at least someone was with me. Now I seemed to be alone. Was I alone? I couldn't be for I had Jesus, and He said He would never leave me nor forsake me.[3]

THE PATH NARROWS

I had crawled as far as I could. But now the passageway had become even narrower—so much so that I was knocking dirt down from the sides and the top. Centipedes and

2 Psalm 23:4 (KJV): "Yea, though I walk through the valley of the shadow of death..."

3 Hebrews 13:5 (NASB): "Make sure that your character is free from the love of money, being content with what you have; for He Himself has said, 'I WILL NEVER DESERT YOU, NOR WILL I EVER ABANDON YOU.'"

nightcrawlers were emerging from the soil. I hoped these insects would not get into my eyes or mouth.

I stopped. I was panting, for there seemed to be less air. Also, it looked like now I would need to lie flat and pull myself along. There did seem to be a number of strong roots that, I felt, I could use as handles to help me drag myself toward the light. I can't tell you how frightening this was.

I thought to myself: "If something enters this tight passageway from the other end, I would be helpless to protect myself." The tightness of the tunnel was terrifying, suffocating. Everything within me was screaming with fear. But there was only one way through—forward.

THE NEST

I arrived at the mouth of a dimly lit, small, cave-like area. Much to my shock and panic, it held some creature's nest. Within the nest was a large egg. It had an enormous Death Adder coiled around it. Where did that egg come from? It looked too large to move through the entryway. How was it to get out? How did something as glorious as a God-infused beneficence get into that leathery snake's egg? Questions assailed me like machine-gun fire.

The Death Adder was sleeping. The suction had increased. I looked to my left to see the origin of the suction, and I saw within the entry two enormous gates opened wide and the tree's bitter taproot plunging through them. "The gates of hell," I whispered to myself. "No wonder the pull is becoming so great." I could hear cries and sounds of torment coming from the yawn of hell itself. I certainly did not want to be dragged in that direction.

I was going to need to awaken the huge snake if I was to retrieve that egg. That much I did realize.

PARALYZED WITH TERROR

I became paralyzed with terror. It dawned on me that more than I myself would bear the consequences of my actions here. I was not a Bible hero. I was not even anointed (at least as far as I could tell). What if I failed? I had seen ministers pass their hand in the air across groups of people and those people fall backward under the power. I'd seen mighty acts done by my fellow Christians, but not one of these acts came from me. Who was I kidding? I could fail. In fact, I probably would fail. "O God," I screamed within myself. "I am endangering thousands of my brothers and sisters because I jumped in and said, 'I'll do this.' Have I lost my mind?"

"Wait a minute, wait a minute," I said to myself. "I'm not going to do this. Jesus is. It is no longer I who lives, but Christ who lives in me.[4] After all, I have been crucified with Christ."[5]

I pulled my focus back to the task. I could see the breathing of the snake. It was huge. I wondered how

4 Galatians 2:20: "I have been crucified with Christ; and it is no longer I who live, but Christ lives in me; and the life which I now live in the flesh I live by faith in the Son of God, who loved me and gave Himself up for me."
5 See Galatians 2:20.

many people it had sunk its fangs into. Did it eat them or just kill them?

But the Lord would not have sent me into this situation if He did not believe that Jesus—with me tagging along—could handle the challenge.

THE DEATH ADDER

I was unnerved, however, by the fact that the snake was an extremely large Death Adder.[6] It was dark, dark gray—to some it might have seemed black. There were faint, lighter gray bands spaced intermittently on its heavy, thick, dangerous looking body. It had a triangular head with ridges above its eyes. I knew it to be part of the cobra family and its bite fatal for anyone far away from an antidote.

I had never seen one so large. What was I saying? I had never seen one at all…only pictures of one. But at this huge size the egg was still too large to have come from the snake. Also, the egg looked as though it had been glued together from smaller egg fragments to protect something or keep it from escaping. Once again I heard a child's whimpering.

"How?" I wondered. "Was there a child within that egg?"

6 Native to Australia, the death adder possesses extremely long fangs in its broad, triangular head. This snake is able to propel its body two to three feet in length at a time, and its venom is extremely poisonous. It eats frogs, lizards, and birds, and does not actively search for prey. The death adder sits in one location and waits for prey to come to it. It has bands of red, brown, and black, with a gray or cream or pink belly. The death adder is a master of camouflage.

The Snake Awakens

The snake slowly opened its eyes. I held very still. I reminded myself that any strike would mean a quick and painful death.

It took a few seconds for the adder to register that someone was in its den. And then it registered that someone was not only in its den but also eyeing its egg. Even though the snake did not lay this egg, he had guarded it long enough to consider it his own. He began to uncoil and rise up.

Up, up it lifted its head, staring at me. I froze under its gaze. Trapped. There was no escape. I had to stand my ground.

Then the snake spoke softly: “Hello, little girl.”

I was stunned. I expected a fight. “Hello,” I answered in as guarded a way as possible.

Lost?

“Lost?” the adder asked kindly.

My breath was coming in short, shallow jerks. I couldn’t seem to answer.

My hand went to the hilt of my sword, and I turned my face to gaze at the mouth of hell, which had begun to throb.

“Oh dear, don’t mind that,” the snake said, indicating the gaping hole.

“It’s hell,” I exclaimed.

“No, no, no,” the snake chuckled. “You think it’s hell

but, just between you and me, there is no hell. It's all bells and whistles meant to scare children and the naïve."

"But..." I gestured toward the agonized sounds.

"Oh." The snake smiled. "Sound effects. It's an elaborate sideshow. You don't actually think a loving God would consign His creation to eternal torment, do you? You are not thinking things through. No—the idea of hell was from folk tales spun by primitive man to scare people into submission."

"But if it's in the Bible, it's true," I said.

"Y-e-s," the snake singsonged as it rocked its head from side to side, "but not in the way you may be understanding it." The snake smiled.

I didn't know what to say. The snake's voice was dripping with honey.

"You must think...better...of your God than to believe stories meant to frighten children." The snake seemed to uncoil itself a little more during this exchange. I crept backward, closer to the mouth of hell.

Coming Closer

"Now, if you are not lost, you must tell me why you have taken all the trouble to come to see me."

I couldn't say the truth, that "I've come to kill you"—but I could speak a truth in answer to the question. "I didn't know you were here." And that was true.

"So you are a curious little girl that struggled to drag

yourself down a dark hole with no one telling you that you were coming to my home?"

"No one told me you were here."

"Surely you asked the One who requires everyone to call Him God Almighty. Pretty arrogant really. But if the kid from Nazareth did nothing without asking His permission—just think of it, as old as He is, and He still can't make His own decisions." He laughed and shook his head. "Everyone must channel Big Daddy—and they call that maturity."

All the while the adder was carefully moving into striking distance, and I was inching away as carefully as I could without being sucked into hell.

"Come now," the snake said with a smile. "You are a guest in my home. You may speak your mind freely. I won't tell you know Who."

A long pause followed as we each calculated the cost of honesty. Finally, I said, "It's true our hope is that we all be one, for our Lord Jesus prayed, 'That they all be one; even as You, Father, are in Me and I in You, that they may also be in Us.'"[7]

---

7 John 17:21–26: "That they may all be one; even as You, Father, are in Me and I in You, that they also may be in Us, so that the world may believe that You sent Me. The glory which You have given Me I have given to them, that they may be one, just as We are one; I in them and You in Me, that they may be perfected in unity, so that the world may know that You sent Me, and loved them, even as You have loved Me. Father, I desire that they also, whom You have given Me, be with Me where I am, so that they may see My glory which You have given Me, for You loved Me before the foundation of the world. O righteous Father, although the world has not known You, yet I have known You; and these have known that You sent Me; and I have made Your name known to them, and will

"And that One is the Big Guy?" he hissed acidly.

"If by the Big Guy you mean God Almighty...yes."

The adder cracked a hard laugh. "Well, He has certainly given Himself an exalted name. So you are willing to give up the control of your own life?"

"Yes, to become one with Him."

"And only do what He does and speak what He speaks... to actually be a puppet mouthing someone else's ideas?"

COMPLETE

"Not a puppet—complete. I love Him, and I want to be as close to Him as I can be. I want union. I want Him to be in me and I in Him. I want Him to speak through me and live through me. I actually want the best for everyone, and the best for them is not me—it's Him."

The snake sneered. "And you think He will give you this? When even the One who called Himself God's Son was begging for it before He died—and He'd known Him a lot longer than either of us?"

As he spoke, the Death Adder had arrived within striking distance. Now I was pressed against one of the open gates to hell. "Stay back," I warned. I drew my sword. Suddenly the sword flashed with a brilliant light. The scriptures on the blade jumped off as if protecting me. This happened in a second, for Christ—our Savior, our Champion, our Warrior King—instantly appeared

---

make it known, so that the love with which You loved Me may be in them, and I in them."

within the dazzling light and removed the snake's head from its body.

He grabbed me with His free hand, sheathed His sword, picked up the egg, and burst through the tunnel, traveling upward.

Bouncing behind us were thousands of silver chains dragging those stuck in the flesh within these roots. Not saved—but it looked as though they were being given another chance on earth to choose Christ. As He exploded from the bowels of the earth, the chains burst into a thousand links of light and then disappeared. Those rescued were scattered across the earth.

"Thank You, Lord," I said.

He smiled down at me. His armor was becoming brighter and brighter as we flew upward. It was as though shards of God's glory were attaching to His armor. Both Jesus' armor and the throne of God began to mirror this incandescent brightness as we drew nearer and nearer to our incomparable and glorious Father.

Chapter 11

THE RETURN

We burst into heaven like the dawning of the first day.

Thousands were standing on the sea of glass. Those nearest the throne stepped back to allow us clear access to our Father. There was great delight in Christ's return—clapping and cheering and some twirling about.

Once our feet touched the crystal sea, we knelt quickly before the Father. Now Jesus' armor shown with incandescent brilliance. My own armor—that which could be seen beneath the drab camel-skin mantle—also shone with a dazzling light.

Before the Throne

As we knelt before the throne, wave upon wave of power and color rolled across all present and continued onward past the throne room. The power was electrifying. The color washed into my mouth and eyes as if invading every part of my body. It was a strange and exhilarating experience.

Jesus placed the egg on the sea of glass before our Father: "Returned," He said.

RUACH

Ruach miraculously appeared. Angels removed the wheat-colored outer garments as He rejoined us.

"Where have you been?" I whispered.

"In you," He whispered back.[1]

"Come," our Father said, "let Me see you." He spoke this to the beneficence as if it were a child.[2]

We remained kneeling before the throne.

Our heavenly Father picked up the egg. A patchwork of discarded snake eggs encased the contents. In His hands the covering burned away, and the contents shone with a brightness that was difficult to express—because of its absolute purity.

"What is this?" I asked Ruach.

"Surpassing Grace," Jesus answered.[3] "It was in Eden when the garden was closed. During the flood it was stolen—only to be returned now."[4]

"It is good to have you back," Ruach said. "The redeemed have need of you."

---

1 The Holy Spirit works within us.

2 A beneficence is a gift of the Father. Grace is of and from God.

3 Surpassing grace is grace that is over and above any of the graces.

4 Surpassing grace is mentioned one time in the Bible. Some of this expansive grace was embraced by the first humans in the garden; otherwise, it would not have been available to mankind all these years. Second Corinthians 9:14: "While they also, by prayer on your behalf, yearn for you because of the surpassing grace of God in you." In the last days however, the fullness of His grace will be needed.

Our heavenly Father held Surpassing Grace before Him, like a daddy holding up a young child. He moved it closer to His face. "Welcome home," He whispered to it.

Those on the sea of glass were enjoying this reunion. He lowered the dazzling light onto His lap. That seemed to be a cue for us to rise.

The First Age of the World

All of us kept our focus on the returned beneficence. I began to think about it. Both this grace and the world were new at the same time. In many ways the beneficence, being locked away, had remained new. It never moved beyond the power and untouched glory of the earth's first age. Even though immensely young, it was likewise immensely powerful because of its purity.

Releasing the Gift

"Even though you have just returned," our Father said, "We must send you out. My children have need of you." He lifted Surpassing Grace before His face and blew on it. Then, instead of releasing it, as I thought He would do, our Father passed it into Himself. This caused an explosion that shook heaven. Out from Him came shiny golden particles that He blew across what looked to be the earth. It was a remarkable experience.

I thought to myself, "How fortunate I am to have seen this dispersion and, even more, to have been a part of the returning of this unbelievable gift that our Father is giving to my spiritual brothers and sisters."

All of this happened so quickly I barely had time to think.

THE FATHER'S GRATITUDE

Jesus smiled at me and squeezed my hand as He returned to His place at the right-hand side of the Father. Ruach bowed at the waist and resumed His position at the left of the Father. The twenty-four Elders, the four living creatures, the cherubs, and seraphim bowed to Them as They took Their proper station by the Father.

I was left standing alone before the throne in our Father's glorious court.

"Thank you, daughter," my Father said.

"Thank You, Daddy, for entrusting to me so important a task."

"Well, now," my Father began. "Are you ready to turn the cloak I gave to you?"

I dropped to my knees again. "Daddy," I whispered. "May I speak to You?"

He leaned forward. "Speak."

"Daddy, I'm so honored to have been given Your mantle, but may I leave it as it is with the drab side out?"

"Drab?" He laughed.

A ripple of twitters moved across the sea of glass.

"Well..." I started to describe it—then thought better of it.

"That's alright, Anna. Proceed."

"Daddy," I sighed. "May we keep the hidden person of my heart between You and me?"

He sat up straight again.

"I am too weak to be known. Let me be hidden in You." I laughed. "I am not being noble, believe me, just—well, realistic."

"Father," Jesus said as He stepped forward. "Allow My sister her request: hiddenness. Her armor is ready and tested for battle. Being unknown and in the place of prayer would help Our cause."

"I concur with this request," the Holy Spirit said. "I have overseen her training, and she is ready for battle."

"You have those who stand with you in this, Anna."

There was a long pause.

"Hiddenness it is," my Father said. It was as if those on the sea of glass exhaled. He continued, "I have kept for Myself thousands who stand with you, unknown, unrecognized by the world and ready to battle through prayer and a godly life. Do you wish to stand with them, Anna?"

"I do, my Lord."

His hands of light came out, and He placed them on my shoulders.

"Receive," He said. The power pouring through Him into my shoulders was so great that I was glad I wasn't standing. When He lifted His hands, I felt a bit woozy.

"Stand, Anna," my Father said.

Both Jesus and the Holy Spirit rushed to my aid, seeing

that I might need help in standing. Each grabbed an arm and lifted me. I was dizzily happy—but trying to clear my head.

My Father continued: "Anna, look to your right." I did so.

It was as though I could see the whole world; millions of Christians clad in armor were standing in readiness.

"Look to your left," He said.

I saw millions more—ready—firm in their resolve.

"Look behind you." The sea of glass was filled with the redeemed in the same armor as mine, smiling—linked in purpose and solidarity.

I looked up to see the thousands of angels flying above our heads. These had shields and javelins.

MUSTERING THE TROOPS

The shofar and thousands of trumpets began to blow.

Jesus said: "We are mustering the troops, Anna."

As I looked, the solidarity and singleness of purpose took my breath away. Here were my brothers and sisters through the ages—all of us—not a single child of God lost, not a single blood-washed believer in Christ missing. Our hearts beat as one: we were of one purpose, one of heart, given to one Commander.

Satan had not stopped our God from building His army, silently, by ones and twos, hidden from sight.

"Are we that near the time of battle?" I asked.

"That near," the Holy Spirit said.

"Daughter, it is time for you to return," my Father said.

"But Daddy, what do You want me to do?" I asked, looking over the marshaled troops.

"Listen for My commands."

I smiled: "I can do that."

My Father rose to His feet. There was absolute silence in heaven.

A brilliant light shone about Jesus.

"Behold!" my Father thundered as He gestured toward Christ: "The Warrior King comes!"

Afterword

This book is somewhat different from the first two books in the trilogy. *The Heavens Opened* and *The Priestly Bride* (now published together under the title *Heaven Awaits the Bride*) were taken down verbatim while I was in heaven in a vision. I asked the Lord if I could look downward in the vision in order to write exactly what I was seeing or what was being said. My heavenly Father granted me this ability. Therefore, by dropping my eyes momentarily, I was able to write and then return to the revelation.

However, this book is different. Originally, I took it from visions, but as I prepared to write the book from the journals, a coven of witches from out of state burned down our home. Most of my journals were spared because they were in fireproof safes, but because I never locked the safes, the journals were water-soaked—but survived. The revelations for the third book in the trilogy were laid out—for I was preparing to write *The Warrior King.*

Therefore, I am writing—like most who have prophetic experiences—from memory. I remember some revelations more clearly than others. The beginning of the book was a vision I had in Kansas City, Missouri, years before I visited heaven. I could not show it all in the book because it was highly detailed as to the horse carts or clothes or expressions on the people's faces, etc. But I remember it as though it were yesterday.

After the house burned, the weight of the revelations continued to concern me because they deal with our greatest enemy—our flesh. For it is the flesh that is attacked and used by the enemy. Therefore, in dealing with the flesh, we also deal with the access given to the demonic in our lives. Truly, I felt obligated to give you what I remembered of that which was given to me. It was meant for you. So obviously the Lord wants you to have it. Also, it was meant to be a help and a blessing to the body of Christ now as well as in the future. It is a gift to you, my brothers and sisters, with whom I will spend eternity.

We may not know each other now—but we will. Oh, what a glorious day that will be when we will know even as we are known. "Now I know in part, but then I will know fully just as I also have been fully known" (1 Cor. 13:12).

I hope this book is a blessing to you. Our heavenly Father wanted you to have it.

Appendix

HOW TO BE BORN AGAIN

When mankind broke covenant with God in the Garden of Eden, the penalty (according to the Lord) was death. Jesus, being a man, represented mankind and paid that price for breaking covenant with God. Through His death, the price was paid—thereby removing the sentence of permanent separation from God that was charged to the human race.

However, now each member of the human race is born in sin (the transgression of divine law). This is true because the sin nature is in our flesh. But God still makes it possible to call the human race.

If a person responds to that call with repentance (deep sorrow for past wrongdoings, even those in our first human family), that person may renounce the sin bringing separation from God due to an atrophied spirit. He or she may ask to be washed clean with the blood of Jesus. In other words, that person may be cleansed by appropriating (that is, to take to oneself or take possession of) the blood of Jesus (eternally shed to remove the death penalty against mankind) and be washed clean.

But our heavenly Father goes further. He offers to us an eternity with Him as a member of His family. When we ask Jesus to come into our hearts and be our life, we are activating Ezekiel 36:26–27: "Moreover, I will give you a new heart and put a new spirit within you; and I will remove the heart of stone from your flesh and give you a heart of flesh. I will put My Spirit within you."

When Jesus said, "I am the way, and the truth, and the life" (John 14:6), He was saying that there is no other way to enter the family of God except through Him. He said that all the Father's truth resides in Him and that the only "life" available is Him.

Therefore, when we repent and then exchange our spiritual death (into which we were born) by asking Jesus to come into our hearts and be our life—we activate the promise in Ezekiel 36:26–27. Our Father cleanses us, puts a new human spirit within us (one alive to God), joins His Spirit to ours, and gives to us a new heart, alive and tender toward God. We are spiritually "born again."

About the Author

After graduating from Baylor University, Anna was awarded top honors in her class at the Royal Academy of Dramatic Art in London. After returning to America, she became an actress in New York City and also began screenwriting. While already cast as Aimee Semple McPherson (the lead in a New York play), she was asked to write the original screenplay for Stephen King's first book, *Carrie*. During the time she was writing the screenplay in East Texas, she became a Christian and married the minister of the church in which she was led to the Lord. (Needless to say, she removed her name from the credits of *Carrie*.)

Together, Anna and her husband experienced a church revival and started a Christian preschool and daycare center, said by state officials to be the best in Texas. She was its headmistress and taught three-year-olds. She also wrote a Texas history book for the Texas Sesquicentennial. The book was accompanied by an audiotape that presented the music for each period of Texas history, with Willie Nelson singing and also reading William Travis' letter from the Alamo.

When they moved to Kansas City, Missouri, Anna helped research the many repentance services that she and her husband coordinated between the pastors and the city's large ethnic population. This included the first repentance service in America between the five chiefs of the First Nations peoples (who once lived in the Kansas City area) and the entire representative pastors from the city. She also headed Kansas City's first March for Jesus.

After they finished their work in Kansas City, the heavens opened for Anna, and she was carried into heaven in the spirit. She recorded in journals every heavenly encounter. Not trusting her memory, she asked the Lord if she could record all that was being said or done while it was happening. She wanted to remember exactly the words of the angels, God the Father, God the Son, and God the Holy Spirit.

Later, the Lord called her to assemble some of the heavenly visits into a book. When halfway through writing the first book, she and her husband moved to the mountains of North Carolina. The first two books, *The Heavens Opened and The Priestly Bride*, are available in one volume titled *Heaven Awaits the Bride*, giving word-for-word literal accounts of Anna's visits to heaven.

The Warrior King, the third book in the trilogy, is taken from revelations that deal with mankind's chief enemy—the flesh—and how our heavenly Father trains us to be warriors for the fierce spiritual battles to come.

Presently, Anna is writing several books, and is also writing a monthly chronicle of the spiritual history of The Moravian Falls House of Prayer, available on the website annarountree.com. This includes the history of the angels assigned to Prayer Mountain.